MORE Children's Sermons to Go

52 Take-Home Lessons About God

VICKY MILLER & DEBORAH RANEY

Illustrations by Vicky, Samantha, & Wesley Miller

Abingdon Press
Nashville

MORE CHILDREN'S SERMONS TO GO:
52 TAKE-HOME LESSONS ABOUT GOD

This book is printed on acid-free paper.

Library of Congress Cataloging-in-Publication Data

Raney, Deborah.
More children's sermons to go : 52 take-home lessons about God / Deborah Raney & Vicky Miller.
p. cm.
Includes indexes.
ISBN 0-687-09962-5 (alk. paper)
1. Children's sermons. 2. Christian education—Home training. 3. Church year sermons. 4. Sermons, American. I. Miller, Vicky, 1956- II. Title.

BV4315 .R36 2001
252'.53—dc21

2001034130

01 02 03 04 05 06 07 08 09 10—10 9 8 7 6 5 4 3 2 1

MANUFACTURED IN THE UNITED STATES OF AMERICA

Lovingly dedicated to our parents,

Max and Winifred Teeter

Acknowledgments

We would like to thank the following people for their assistance with this book:

Those who have so graciously lent us their ideas: author Emilie Barnes; George Beyer; Frances Davies; Sheila DeGarmo; Dorie Kloss; Judi Webster; Jeanne Wildin; and our parents, Max and Winifred Teeter.

The Reverend Jeff Miller, of Mitchell Chapel United Methodist Church, Hutchinson, Kansas, whose insight and theological advice were much appreciated.

Our husbands and children, for their patience while we worked on the manuscript, and for giving us an opportunity to put these lessons to the test.

And the children of our churches, who are always eager and willing to learn and to teach us.

"But Jesus said, 'Let the little children come to me. Don't stop them, because the kingdom of heaven belongs to people who are like these children.'" (Matthew 19:14)

Contents

Introduction

Through many years of presenting children's messages in our own churches, we have discovered that a small trinket to carry away from the children's sermon becomes a highly effective reminder of the lesson throughout the week. A simple memento can serve as a reminder for the whole family to talk about at home.

The take-home items can also be adapted for craft projects in Christian education classes or children's church. And while we believe the "take-home" angle is a very effective one, many of these sermons may be easily tailored for use without the take-home treat. To that end, the *You will need* section at the beginning of each sermon lists only the items necessary for the presentation of the lesson itself. If additional items are needed for the take-home treat, they are listed in the *To take home* section.

It is our hope that the ideas in this book will be a starting point for your own creativity. In writing these lessons we have targeted children ages three to ten, but our own audiences have ranged from two-year-olds to preadolescents. You will best know the way to tailor these messages to your particular audience.

When the first edition of *Children's Sermons to Go* was published in 1998, we began to hear that many parents were using the book for family devotions. Indeed, many of these lessons can be easily adapted for a family setting, and the take-home item at the end of each sermon can become a craft project or snack item that the entire family may enjoy. We are thrilled that parents have discovered this creative way of using the book. We trust that *More Children's Sermons to Go* will provide families, as well as those who present children's messages in their churches, with even more innovative ways to demonstrate and instill God's truths.

May you be blessed as you serve God through the infinitely important calling of sharing Christian truths with precious little ones.

Vicky Miller

Deborah Raney

Note: As always, in working with children in any setting, safety is a primary concern. Because some of the take-home treats we suggest are edible, please be mindful of any special dietary needs represented among the children of your church. It is important to have an alternative item available for those who might be allergic to—or unable to eat—the planned treat.

1

A Firm Foundation

You will need:
- a set of building blocks

Scripture: (Matthew 7:24) *"Everyone who hears these things I say and obeys them is like a wise man. The wise man built his house on rock."*

[Make a tower by stacking building blocks. The higher and more precarious the tower, the better. Consider asking a few of the older children to help stack the blocks very carefully.] Well, we have built quite a tall tower, haven't we? Good job, kids. Now, what do you think would happen if I moved this bottom block just a teeny, tiny bit? Do you think our tower would keep standing? Let's try it and see. I'll just move it a little bit. *[Move a key block just enough so that the entire tower tumbles.]*

Wow! To think I moved just one little block a tiny bit, and it made the whole tower come crashing down. If we were to talk to a carpenter—someone who knows all about building things—he would tell us that the foundation—the bottom part of the building that all the rest of the building stands on—is the most important part of all. If the foundation shifts even a few inches, the whole building will become weaker. And if the foundation shifts a great deal (as it might in an earthquake), the whole building may come tumbling down just like these blocks did.

The Bible tells us that we should build our lives on the foundation of Jesus Christ. The Bible calls Jesus the Cornerstone. The cornerstone of a building is the point of the foundation that the rest of the building is built from. If the cornerstone is strong and straight and true, the rest of the building will be strong and straight and true as well.

The Bible teaches us that Jesus is the truth, so there is nothing stronger that we could build our lives on. And how do we do that? How do we build our lives on Jesus? By following Jesus' teaching and the example of his life.

To take home: Give each child a building block or a simple block of wood on which you have written the scripture verse.

2

A Permanent Solution

You will need:

- writing tablet
- a permanent marker
- an eraser

Scripture: (Proverbs 3:3) *Don't ever stop being kind and truthful. Let kindness and truth show in all you do. Write them down in your mind as if on a tablet.*

[With permanent marker write the words "kind" and "truthful" on a tablet.] I've written two words on this tablet. Can anyone tell me what the words are? I have an eraser with me. Would you *[choose a child]* try to erase these words for me, please? You aren't able to erase the words, are you? The marker I used is a permanent marker, so that means anything you write with this marker is on there for good.

Listen to this Bible verse from Proverbs 3. The heading in my Bible says that this is advice to children, so you should listen very carefully. *[Read scripture.]* Just as I wrote on this tablet with a permanent marker that will always be there, so are we to always think about being kind and truthful in all we do.

What are some of the things that we

do each day? *[Suggest answers such as go to school, play with friends, play sports, help Mom or Dad.]* In all of these things that we do in our lives, the Bible says we are to be kind and truthful. How could we be this way at school? *[Be kind to the teacher and the workers at school, as well as to the other kids; do not cheat on schoolwork, and so forth.]* How can we be kind and truthful with our friends? *[By letting them have their way sometimes and by always being honest.]* What about in sports? When we get caught up in winning, isn't it sometimes hard to be a good sport and to be kind and truthful during the game? We may be tempted to be rude to members of the other team. But remember that scripture says we are to be kind and truthful in all we do. What about being kind and truthful when helping our parents? How could we do that? *[Don't argue or complain when our parents ask us to do a job, for example.]* It would be kind to do the job willingly, wouldn't it? And we can be truthful by doing our very best job at anything we are asked to do and by not taking shortcuts.

To take home: Write the words "kind" and "truthful" on the cover or the first page of small tablets. Give one to each child.

Bear One Another's Burdens

You will need:

- a basketful of stuffed teddy bears
- two Bibles (a King James Version and the *New Living Translation*)

Scripture: (Galatians 6:2 KJV) *Bear ye one another's burdens, and so fulfil the law of Christ.*

[Read the scripture from the King James Version of the Bible.] This verse from Galatians is from a very old Bible called the King James Version. I like it because it uses the word "bear," and, as you can see, I like bears! I brought a whole basket of bears with me today to help us remember this scripture. The verse tells us to "bear one another's burdens." But what does that mean? Burdens are problems and feelings that weigh us down and make us sad or tired. And the word "bear" here isn't like the fuzzy kind of bears I have in my basket. The word "bear" means to "hold up" or "carry." This is how that scripture reads in a newer translation of the Bible: "Share each other's troubles and problems" (NLT). So to bear

each other's troubles and problems means to *share* each other's troubles and problems, doesn't it?

But how can you share someone's problems with him or her? Do you have any ideas? What if one of your friends is having trouble with a bully on the way home from school? How could you share his problem? Maybe you could walk home with him and help him stand up to the bully. Maybe you could go with him to talk to a teacher or another adult who could help. And what if one of your friends is feeling very sad because her dog or cat died? How could you bear—or share—her troubles? Maybe you could do that just by being a good listener. It might make her feel better just to remember what a wonderful pet she had. Or maybe you've lost a pet, and you remember how sad you felt when that happened. You might even be able to help your friend find a new pet when she's ready. When someone is going through a tough time, it helps to know that he or she is not alone.

Sharing our troubles with each other is a good way to make big troubles seem much smaller. And God wants each one of us to be a good trouble "share-er"—or "bear-er"!

To take home: Give each child a tiny stuffed toy bear. "When you look at this bear I hope you will remember that we are supposed to 'bear' each other's troubles."

Note: Miniature stuffed bears are available inexpensively from discount or party supply stores or catalogs.

Blind Faith

You will need:

- a clean bicycle

Scripture: (Psalm 48:14) *This God is our God forever and ever. He will guide us from now on.*

This morning, I brought a bicycle to church. We don't see bicycles in the sanctuary very often, do we? But I think this bicycle can help us learn a very important lesson. Would one of you like to volunteer to ride this bike down the aisle? *[If there are only a few children, let each have a quick turn. Otherwise, choose one of the older, more responsible children or ask a young preteen from the congregation to volunteer.]*

Okay, what I want you to do is ride this bicycle down the aisle and back in as straight a line as possible. *[Beforehand, enlist people seated on the aisles to help in avoiding a crash. When the child successfully completes the ride, say:]* You did a great job. But now I'm going to ask you to do it again, only this time you will be blindfolded! Would you like someone to help guide you along? *[If the child says "no," let him or her try the ride alone. But after the blindfold is on,*

put a folding chair in the path. Walk next to the rider with a hand on the bike seat. When the child crashes into the chair, ask again if he or she would like a guide. The guide should help him or her ride to the end of the aisle.]

Okay, leave the bike there and let's come back to the front. You know, riding this bicycle blindfolded is a little bit like our lives. We can't always see what's ahead of us or what our future will bring. That's why God put parents, teachers, pastors, and others in our lives—to guide us so we won't have any serious "crashes." As much as we sometimes want to do things our own way, God knows that children sometimes need help in making good choices. And even when we are grown up, we will still need God's help to guide us in life.

To take home: Make handlebar streamers for each child to take home and decorate his or her bicycle with. These can be made by cutting ten to fifteen strips of plastic "crepe" paper that measure twelve inches. Double the strips and wrap the folded center neatly with clear mailing tape to form a "pom-pom."

Buried Treasure

You will need:

- a low-sided box half full of sand, in which you have buried small toys or trinkets

Scripture: (Matthew 13:44) *"The kingdom of heaven is like a treasure hidden in a field. One day a man found the treasure, and then he hid it in the field again. The man was very happy to find the treasure. He went and sold everything that he owned to buy that field."*

We are going to hunt for hidden treasure this morning. I'll give each of you a chance to dig in the sand for a treasure. *[Let each child dig through the sand until he or she finds a trinket to keep.]*

In our scripture reading today we are told about a man who finds a hidden treasure. *[Read scripture.]* People who study and write about the Bible believe that this man probably was not looking for treasure. He was probably just going about his everyday business when he accidentally came across the treasure. In Jesus' time people often buried treasures. They did have places like banks back in those days, but ordinary people couldn't use them. That's why they buried their valuable belongings in the ground. There were many wars that took place in the land where Jesus lived. So when people were afraid a war was about to break out, they would bury anything they owned of value, hoping to dig it up when the war was over.

Jesus said that the kingdom of heaven is like a treasure hidden in a field. Having Jesus in our hearts is worth more than anything else in the whole world. Just like the man who sold all that he owned to buy the field with the treasure, we should be willing to give up all the things that seem important to us—our toys, our games, the time we spend watching TV or playing with friends—in order to have Jesus in our hearts.

To take home: Let each child take home the trinket he or she found in the sand.

Camping Out

You will need:

- a bag of large marshmallows
- various camping supplies
- if possible, a small pop-up tent
- perhaps a "campfire" (cover two or three flashlights with red cellophane, turn on flashlights, and lay small branches on top to give the effect of a fire)

Scripture: (2 Corinthians 4:18–5:1) *So we set our eyes not on what we see but on what we cannot see. What we see will last only a short time. But what we cannot see will last forever. We know that our body—the tent we live in here on earth—will be destroyed. But when that happens, God will have a house for us to live in. It will not be a house made by men. It will be a home in heaven that will last forever.*

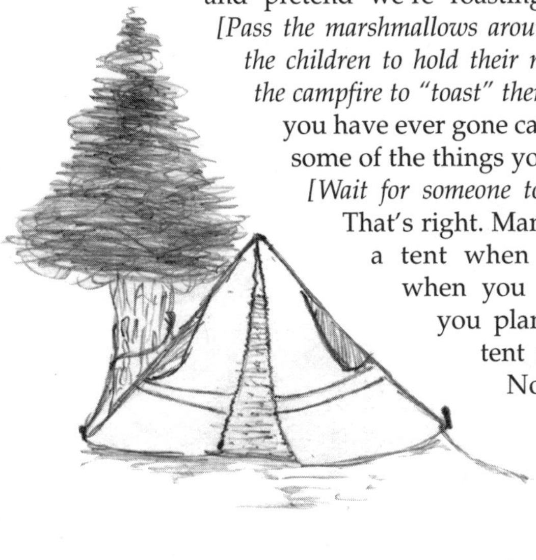

Today we're going to pretend that we're on a camping trip. We can sit around the campfire and pretend we're roasting marshmallows. *[Pass the marshmallows around. You might tell the children to hold their marshmallows over the campfire to "toast" them.]* How many of you have ever gone camping? What are some of the things you took with you? *[Wait for someone to mention a tent.]* That's right. Many times you take a tent when you camp. But when you go camping, do you plan to live in your tent for a long time? No. Usually, the tent is only your home for a few days or weeks, isn't it? In 2 Corinthians, Paul talks about a tent. He calls the body "the tent we live in here on earth." Living eighty or ninety years here on earth may seem like a long time to us, but to God it's just like going on a weekend camping trip. Our real home is in heaven. God has made a home for us there that will last forever. Paul says we should set our eyes not on what we see, but on what we cannot see. We should take care of our bodies, but we shouldn't be overly concerned about fixing up the tents—or bodies—that are just going to get old and will someday be destroyed. Paul goes on to say that our only goal is to please God. God gave us these bodies to use and enjoy, but the important thing is that we make God happy in everything we do.

To take home: Give each child one more marshmallow to take back to his or her seat.

7

Chips and Cracks

You will need:

- enough imperfect—but still usable and attractive—teacups for each child to have one (garage sales and flea markets usually offer an abundance of inexpensive dishes)
- one cup that is damaged too badly to be used for drinking (use this cup to hold a small plant or pencils or candies)
- a teapot filled with water

Scripture: (2 Corinthians 12:10) *So I am happy when I have weaknesses, insults, hard times, sufferings, and all kinds of troubles. All these things are for Christ. And I am happy, because when I am weak, then I am truly strong.*

[Pour a small amount of water into each child's teacup. When the children are finished drinking, instruct them to study the cups in their hands.] These cups are all very pretty, aren't they? Each one is different, and each one has a special beauty about it. But if you look closely, you will see that none of these cups is perfect. Every cup has a chip or a scratch or a broken handle.

In a way, you and I are like these teacups. Each one of us has something in our life that we'd like to change. Maybe we're not as smart as we'd like to be. Maybe we can't run as fast as our classmates. Maybe there is something we'd like to change about our bodies.

Or maybe we have problems in our families, or something happened in our lives that hurt us and made us sad. But when God looks at us, God sees that even with all our problems and imperfections, we are beautiful and useful. In fact, the Bible teaches that God's power is actually stronger when we are weak!

[Hold up the most damaged cup.] Even this cup, so badly damaged that it will no longer hold water, is still very useful. In fact, it makes a perfect holder for this plant (these pencils, or whatever.) No matter who we are or what troubles life has given us, God loves us and wants us to do good things in Jesus' name.

To take home: Let each child take home the cup he or she drank from as a reminder that God loves each one of us in spite of our imperfections.

8

Crossing the Bridge

You will need: [If you do not use the take-home item, you will not need any materials to present this lesson.]

Scripture: (John 14:6) *Jesus answered, "I am the way. And I am the truth and the life. The only way to the Father is through me."*

[If your church has a platform or stage, you could stand on stage and challenge the children to join you. If you don't have such a platform, use the aisle as the dividing line. You might lay a piece of string across the aisle to make the line obvious.]

I'd like to play a little game with you this morning. I'm going to stand on the stage, and I want each of you to try to get up here beside me. But there are a couple of rules you must follow. First of all, you may not touch the stairs. And second, you may not walk, run, crawl, or scoot. Those rules make it pretty tough, don't they? Does it sound impossible? Well, let's think about it. Can you think of any way at all that you could get up here without touching the stairs and without walking, running, crawling, or scooting?

[If the children don't offer their own ideas or come

up with the right answer, give them hints.] Let's think about it. Maybe you need some help. How might someone else help you get up here? What if your mom, dad, or a friend carried you up here? Would that work? Your feet wouldn't touch the stairs, would they? And you wouldn't be walking or crawling or breaking any of the other rules. Sounds as if that's the answer, doesn't it?

[Move down to the same level or side of the aisle as the children.] You know, our relationship with God is a lot like this game. There are directions in God's Word about how we can get to heaven to be with God. The Bible tells us that we can't get there by ourselves. We can't get there just by being a good person. We can't get there just because we grew up in a Christian family. No, according to the Bible, there is only one way to get to God and that is by faith in Jesus Christ. Only by trusting in Jesus as our Savior can we truly know God.

To take home: Cut thick crosses from heavy paper and write "Jesus" in bold letters across the horizontal bar. Tell the children that these crosses should serve as reminders that Jesus is the only "bridge" we can cross to get to God.

9

Jesus Never Says "Do Not Disturb"

You will need:

- a "Do not disturb" door hanger.

Scripture: (Mark 6:30-34) *The apostles that Jesus had sent out to preach returned. They gathered around him and told him about all the things they had done and taught. Crowds of people were coming and going. Jesus and his followers did not even have time to eat. He said to them, "Come with me. We will go to a quiet place to be alone. There we will get some rest." So they went in a boat alone to a place where there were no people. But many people saw them leave and recognized them. So people from all the towns ran to the place where Jesus was going. They got there before Jesus arrived. When he landed, he saw a great crowd waiting. Jesus felt sorry for them, because they were like sheep without a shepherd. So he taught them many things.*

How many of you have ever had a house full of company? Maybe you had Christmas or Thanksgiving at your house. Or maybe your parents had a party. After the people have been at your house a long time, and it is noisy and crowded and you are getting tired, what do you feel like doing? Unless you really like parties, you may want to go in your bedroom or another quiet room in the house, shut the door, and be by yourself. Maybe you'd want to hang a sign like this on your door so no one would bother you. *[Show children the take-home item.]*

Jesus felt like that at times. We are told in Mark 6 about a time when so many people were coming to Jesus that he and his disciples didn't even have a chance to eat. Jesus told his disciples to go with him to a quiet place so they could rest. They got in a boat and went to a private place. But people saw them leaving and ran ahead on land to where Jesus was going. When the boat landed, Jesus saw a large crowd waiting. How would you feel if you were Jesus? Maybe you'd say "I wish these people would go away. Don't they know I need my sleep?" Maybe you'd even be tempted to get back in your boat and sail away from the people.

But this was not what Jesus did. Jesus felt sorry for them because they were like sheep without a shepherd. Even though he was tired and hungry, Jesus took time for the people and taught them many things because he loved them.

Jesus will always have time for us. We can call on him any time of the day or night and he will be there for us. Jesus will never say, "Do not disturb."

To take home: Ask for "Do not disturb" door hangers from a motel. Above the words "Do not disturb," glue a piece of paper or label on which you have written: "Jesus will never say."

10

First Things First

You will need:

- a baby doll
- various clothing for the doll (undershirt, outfit, diaper, shoes, and socks)

Scripture: (Matthew 6:33) *"The thing you should want most is God's kingdom and doing what God wants. Then all these other things you need will be given to you."*

I brought my favorite doll to church this morning. Well, you know how it is on Sunday mornings with everyone rushing around, trying to get ready on time. I didn't have time to get her dressed. So I put her clothes in a bag and brought them with me. While we talk this morning, I'll get her ready for church.

[Begin dressing the doll in reverse order: the nightgown or outfit, then shoes, socks, undershirt, and finally, the diaper. As the children begin to notice that you are not doing this task correctly, ask for their ideas on why things should be done differently.]

So you don't think I did a very good job of dressing this doll? But she has all of her clothes on. See? She has everything she needs: a little outfit, an undershirt to keep her warm, shoes, socks, and a diaper. Isn't that everything?

Oh, you think I didn't put things on in the right order? Well, you are right. Even though this baby has everything she needs, putting them on in this order won't work out well at all because I didn't put first things first.

You see, sometimes it is very important to do one thing before another and to get things in exactly the right order. The Bible tells about a time when Jesus' friends must have been worrying about things such as what they would eat or what they would wear. Jesus told them not to worry about those things. Instead, he told them that if they would look to God's kingdom—and the right ways of doing things—first, then all those other things would fall into place. If we learn and practice the things God has told us, then everything else we need in life will be given to us at just the right time and in just the right way.

To take home: Cut out simple paper dolls from heavy paper. From thinner paper, cut an outfit for each doll. You could use outfits cut from catalogs or magazines. Give these to the children as reminders that God will take care of all of our needs if we look after the important things—God and God's kingdom—first.

11

How Does Your Garden Grow?

You will need:

- a few plants and flowers in pots

Scripture: (Colossians 1:9, 10) *Since the day we heard this about you, we have continued praying for you. We ask God that you will know fully what God wants. We pray that you will also have great wisdom and understanding in spiritual things. Then you will live the kind of life that honors and pleases the Lord in every way. You will produce fruit in every good work and grow in the knowledge of God.*

It won't be long before we plant our gardens and put new flowers in the flowerpots on our porches and patios. Let's think for a minute about how we plant our gardens and our flowerpots. First, we plant the seeds in the ground or put small seedlings into a pot. What do we do after that? That's right. We have to give them water. We have to be sure to pull the weeds out of the soil so that they don't choke the new plants. What else? We might need to give the plants fertilizer or put a special spray on them to keep away the bugs.

As the summer goes on, we watch our plants grow and mature, and finally, we get to enjoy the crop. We might get to eat the vegetables we grew, or we might get to bring a pretty bouquet of the flowers to the dinner table.

But what would happen if we planted the seeds or seedlings and then just ignored them? In the garden, the weeds would probably just take over, wouldn't they? We would go looking for our tomatoes and all we would find would be tall, tough weeds. We might go to pick a flower from our flowerpot and find that the soil was dry and cracked and that the green plant had died of thirst before it ever got even one blossom on it.

The same thing is true of our life with Jesus. When we learn a few things about God, it's as though a tiny seed is planted in our hearts. But we need to continue to nurture that seed and take care of it so it will grow and bear fruit. By bearing fruit, I mean putting the things we learn about God into practice. Jesus Christ wants to live inside our hearts and help us grow into strong Christian boys and girls. How can we take care of the seed of faith that God has planted in us? One way is by praying for ourselves and others. A second way is by coming to church and Sunday school. A third way is by doing kind things for others. And the most important way we can grow is by reading the Bible and obeying what it says.

To take home: Give each child a single flower as a reminder that if we are to blossom and bear fruit, we must take care of the garden of our heart. (Even in the winter, daisies and carnations are quite inexpensive.)

12

I Am the Vine

You will need:

- a branch from an apple tree (Many orchards are happy to supply one, especially during pruning season.)
- a basket of apples (With nontoxic marker, write one of the following words on each one: *love, joy, peace, patience, kindness, goodness, faithfulness, gentleness, self-control.*)

Scripture: (John 15:5) *"I am the vine, and you are the branches. If a person remains in me and I remain in him, then he produces much fruit. But without me he can do nothing."*

I visited an apple orchard this week, and I brought two things home with me: this branch that the orchard workers cut from an apple tree, and this basket of beautiful apples. Don't they look delicious? This branch had apples growing on it just a few weeks ago, but then the workers in the orchard cut the branch off. Did you know that in the Bible Jesus calls us branches? Jesus tells us that he is the vine and we are the branches. The Bible says that if we stay close to Jesus, we will bear much fruit. Now do you think that means that if we love Jesus, apples and pears and peaches will start growing out of our ears? No, I don't think so. But what could Jesus have meant by this?

Well, there is another scripture that tells us exactly what the fruit Jesus was talking about is. Galatians 5 tells us about some-

thing called the *fruit of the spirit*. This isn't the kind of fruit we eat. Instead, the fruit of the spirit is the good qualities that Jesus wants each of us to have—qualities such as love, joy, peace, patience, kindness, goodness, faithfulness, gentleness, and self-control. These are things that we just can't get unless we stay close to Jesus.

Take a look at this branch. When all the apple trees blossom next spring, do you think this branch will have any flowers on it? Why not? Because it didn't stay close to the tree. The tree has roots that go deep into the soil to carry water and nutrients to all the branches so that they can grow apples. Jesus is our "tree"—the one that helps us grow good fruit. Unless we stay close to Jesus, we can't have the kind of fruit he wants us to grow—love, joy, peace, and all of the other fruits of the Spirit that we talked about.

To take home: Let each child choose an apple from the basket as a reminder of the kinds of fruit that Jesus wants us to "grow."

I'm with Him

You will need:
- an official admittance badge from a hospital or business

Scripture: (Acts 4:12) *"Jesus is the only One who can save people. His name is the only power in the world that has been given to save people. And we must be saved through him!"*

Have you ever visited a hospital or maybe your mom's or dad's office building where the people who worked in the building had to wear a special badge showing that they belonged there? Many times, these places will not allow anyone in the building without an official badge like this. *[Show the children your badge and explain the reason for this particular one.]* If you or I just walked into the building, a security guard would probably tell us that we had to leave because we were not wearing a badge. But we might be able to go to the main office and request a badge that would allow us to get into the building.

Sometimes, we might need to stick with a person who was wearing a badge. If the security guard asked us where our badge was, we could just point to the person we were with and say "I'm with her." The security guard might look at that person, see that she had the necessary badge, and say, "Oh, you're with her? Then that's fine. Go right on in."

Well, did you know that when we

have Jesus living in our hearts, it's a little bit like having a badge that gets us into heaven? The Bible tells us that there is no other name on earth or in heaven that will get us "admitted" to heaven. We can't say, "Oh, well, my mom and dad know Jesus, so please let me in" or "Well, I know Pastor Jones, and he knows Jesus, so please let me in." No, the Bible says that the only way we can get into heaven is knowing and serving Jesus ourselves. That is how we can have the promise of a home in heaven someday. If we know Jesus, it's a little bit like wearing a badge. God sees that our "badge" came straight from Jesus and says "Oh, you're with him? Then that's fine. Go right on in."

To take home: Make badges for each child to take home. You might use self-adhesive paper nametags or "official" plastic badges with pin backs, both of which can be purchased in an office supply store. On the badge write: "Please admit. Official guest of Jesus."

14

Living Faith

You will need:

- a battery-operated toy, such as a remote control car or truck
- batteries to operate the toy

Scripture: (James 2:14-17) *My brothers, if someone says he has faith, but does nothing, his faith is worth nothing. Can faith like that save him? A brother or sister in Christ might need clothes or might need food. And you say to him, "God be with you! I hope you stay warm and get plenty to eat." You say this, but you do not give that person the things he needs. Unless you help him, your words are worth nothing. It is the same with faith. If faith does nothing, then that faith is dead, because it is alone.*

I brought this neat car with me this morning. It is operated by remote control. We could have a lot of fun with this. *[Try to operate the car without the batteries.]* Hmm, something is wrong. This car isn't doing a thing. Are any of you mechanics? What do you think the problem could be? *[Someone may suggest that it has no batteries. If not, open the compartment where the batteries go and show the children the problem.]* This reminds me of something that James talks about in the Bible. *[Read scripture.]* James says that our faith is dead without actions, just as this car is dead without the batteries. Now, let's put some batteries into this car and see what happens. *[Put the batteries in place*

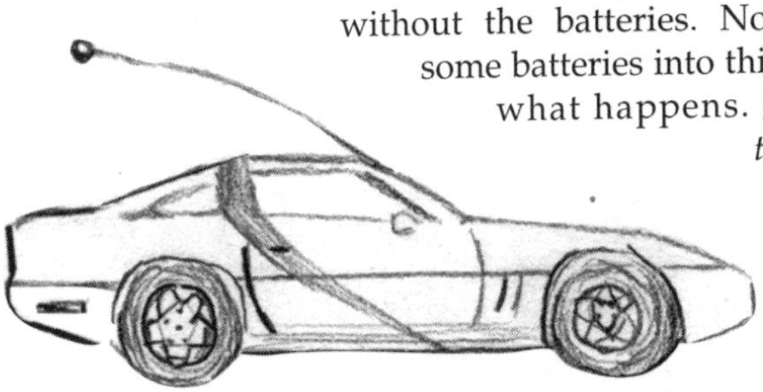

and run the car.] Great! It's running the way it should. So just like these batteries cause the car to come alive, our good actions toward others make our faith a living faith.

To take home: Give each child an inexpensive miniature car or truck to take home, telling them, "These little cars don't run on batteries. But maybe when you play with them this week, they will remind you of this morning's lesson."

15

Is That Your Final Answer?

You will need:

- two pretend checks made out for a million dollars paid to the order of "Child of God"

Scripture: (Genesis 9:16) *"When the rainbow appears in the clouds, I will see it. Then I will remember the agreement that continues forever. It is between me and every living thing on the earth."*

[Read scripture.] In the scripture we just read, we heard about a covenant that God made with Noah. Who can tell me what a covenant is? All right, I'll help you out a little. You've all probably seen the game show "Who Wants to Be a Millionaire?" *[Hold up one of the pretend checks. Choose one child to be the first contestant.]* Would you like to play that game? Okay, first question: Is a covenant: (*a*) an ant's home, (*b*) a small blanket, (*c*) an agreement, or (*d*) wanting what belongs to someone else? *[Call on one child.]* So you think the answer is c? Is that your final answer? Well, you're absolutely right! A covenant is an agreement. And God made an agreement with Noah. Do you remember what that agreement was? God said that he would never again destroy all life on earth with a

flood. And God gave a sign to go along with that agreement. What was that sign? *[Choose another child, and if he or she answers correctly, give him or her the second pretend check.]* Was it: (*a*) lightning, (*b*) doves, (*c*) butterflies, or (*d*) a rainbow? *[Call on a child.]* Is that your final answer? Yes, the answer is d, a rainbow. God said, "When the rainbow appears in the clouds, I will see it. Then I will remember the agreement that continues forever. It is between me and every living thing on earth." The rainbow reminds us of God's mercy and grace. It reminds us that God loves us and is good to us even when we don't deserve it.

There is another sign that reminds us of God's mercy and grace. You can look around this sanctuary and see it. Has anyone found it yet? Yes, it's the cross. The cross reminds us of a new covenant, or agreement, that Jesus brought from God to us. Jesus willingly died on the cross to take away our sins and to give us life that will go on forever. The cross reminds us that, even when we don't deserve it, Jesus loved us enough to die for us so that we could live with God forever. And that should make us all feel like millionaires!

To take home: Duplicate a million-dollar check for each child. Decorate the checks with rainbow and/or cross stickers to remind the children of the promise that should make us feel like millionaires. (Or draw a picture of a rainbow and let each child take home a copy to color during the week.)

16

Leave a Message After the Beep

You will need:

- a telephone
- recordings of a busy signal and an answering machine message saying the following: "I'm sorry but I can't answer the phone right now. Please leave a message after the beep and I'll get back to you one of these days."

Scripture: (Romans 10:13, 14 NLT) *For "Anyone who calls on the name of the Lord will be saved." But how can they call on him to save them unless they believe in him? And how can they believe in him if they have never heard about him? And how can they hear about him unless someone tells them?*

Telephones are an important part of our lives, aren't they? It seems as if we use the telephone every single day. And if anything ever happens to our phone, we hardly know how to get along without it. Now, with answering machines, we can use the telephone even when there is nobody home on the other end!

Have you ever thought what it would be like if we could dial a number and reach God on the other end? What if we called God and this happened? *[Play the recording of the busy signal.]* Or what if we called God and got an answering machine? *[Play the answering machine*

recording.] How would you feel if you got a message like that when you tried to "call" God?

Well, I'm happy to report that we can call on God any time of the day or night and never, ever get a busy signal or an answering machine message. God is just a prayer away and will always hear us when we pray. *[Read the first verse of the scripture.]*

But this telephone reminds me of another important part of that scripture. *[Read the rest of the scripture.]* God wants us to share the good news of God's love—the good news of Jesus—with people who don't know God. Some people have never heard the wonderful news that they can call on Jesus any time of day or night. I hope you will remember that you can call on Jesus in prayer any time at all, and I also hope that you will share this good news with others.

To take home: Cut out telephone shapes on which you have printed the scripture. Office supply stores sometimes carry notepads decorated with drawings of telephones.

17

Light and Shadow

You will need:

- a small paper-doll shape cut from heavy paper (a gingerbread cookie cutter makes a good template if you're not an artist)
- a flashlight or small lamp
- a ruler or yardstick

Scripture: (Philippians 4:13) *I can do all things through Christ because he gives me strength.*

Today I want to show you how Jesus can help us do great things when we stay close to him. I brought this cardboard cutout of a person with me. Now this person doesn't look very big, does he? Let's measure him. Look at that. He's only about six inches high.

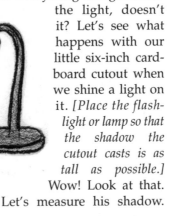

Now, I'm about five feet seven inches. Do any of you know how tall you are? Four feet three inches? Four feet ten inches? But have you ever walked under a streetlamp at night and watched your shadow grow taller and taller? Everything changes under the light, doesn't it? Let's see what happens with our little six-inch cardboard cutout when we shine a light on it. *[Place the flashlight or lamp so that the shadow the cutout casts is as tall as possible.]* Wow! Look at that. Let's measure his shadow.

This light makes the tiny cardboard man seem almost twice as tall as he really is.

This reminds me of the way Jesus helps us do big things for him. We may not be four feet tall, but when we let the light of Jesus shine on us, he helps us do great things. Can you think of some ways Jesus might help us do something big for him?

How about visiting an older person in the hospital or nursing home? It might not seem like such a big deal to us, but I'm sure that a lonely, hurting, or sick person thinks it is a very big deal to get a visit from a smiling young face like yours. What about helping your mom or your dad with a job they need to have done? It might be something small like washing the supper dishes, but the extra time it will give your parents to do something else will give them much joy.

The Bible tells us that Jesus is the light of the world. When we let him shine on us, even the small things we do for others can seem bigger than we ever imagined.

To take home: Give each child a cutout identical to the one you used. You might cut the shapes from shiny, reflective paper to represent the light of Jesus.

Mirror, Mirror

You will need:

- one hand mirror, which the children may pass around and share

Scripture: (Matthew 7:12*a*) *"Do for other people the same things you want them to do for you."*

I hope this mirror will help us understand an important lesson from God's Word. What happens when you look in the mirror and smile? Does the face in the mirror smile back at you? What if you say "hello" to the person you see there? He or she says hello back, right? But what if you frown at that person or make a mean face? You get the same frown or mean face in return, don't you?

There is a very important scripture in the Bible that is called the Golden Rule. This verse is found in Matthew 7:12 and this is what it says: *[Read scripture.]* What this means is that God wants us to treat others the way we would like to be treated. The exciting thing about this scripture is that just as the face in the mirror copied the face that we "gave" it, other people usually copy the face we give them. What usually happens when we give someone a smile? That's right! We get a smile back, don't we? But if we

frown at someone or make a mean face at them, most often we will get a frown right back. That just seems to be the way it is. Wouldn't it be wonderful if everyone in our church tried his or her very best to give only smiles to other people this morning? If that happened, I think we'd all leave here feeling better than when we came. And what if we took our smiles out with us and gave them to the people on the street on our way home, to the people in our families, or to the children and teachers we will see at school tomorrow? And what if we took it one step further and decided to treat everyone as nicely as we want to be treated? We could be kind to everyone and speak only encouraging words. It's not hard to imagine that pretty soon our whole city would be smiling and being nice to one another! And all because a few of us decided to practice the Golden Rule. I hope that each time we see our face reflected in the mirror, we'll remember that a simple smile can make someone else so happy that they'll want to pass it on and on and on. And just think what a better place this world would be if that happened!

To take home: Give each child a small mirror to take home. Mirrors may be purchased inexpensively at discount stores, beauty supply stores, or through carnival supply catalogs.

19

More Than Meets the Eye

You will need:

- a piece of paper on which you have drawn a picture using "invisible ink" (see instructions below)
- a lamp with a 60 or 75 watt lightbulb (remove the shade)

Scripture: (Luke 17:20, 21) *Some of the Pharisees asked Jesus, "When will the kingdom of God come?" Jesus answered, "God's kingdom is coming, but not in a way that you will be able to see with your eyes. People will not say, 'Look, God's kingdom is here!' or, 'There it is!' No, God's kingdom is within you."*

[Turn on the lamp so the bulb can heat up while you talk. Show the children the piece of paper on which you have written or drawn using "invisible ink." You can do this by writing with a toothpick or cotton swab dipped in lemon juice. Let the juice dry beforehand. Holding the paper over the lightbulb will cause the message to become visible. (Caution: the lightbulb will become very hot.)]

What do you see? Nothing? Are you sure? Watch what happens when I hold the paper up to this light. There is a hidden picture, isn't there?

There were some people in Jesus' time called the Pharisees who just didn't understand Jesus. When Jesus talked, it was as if they were looking at a blank piece of paper and couldn't see the hidden picture.

Jesus told them, "God's kingdom is coming, but not in a way that you will be able to see with your eyes." People would not be able to point to a city or a fort or an army of soldiers and say, "Look, here is God's kingdom!" Instead, Jesus meant that his kingdom was made up of people—people who have Jesus in their hearts.

In the same way that we could not see the hidden picture without holding it up to the light, the Pharisees could not picture a kingdom they could not see or touch. But Jesus said, "God's kingdom is within you." God's kingdom is like the hidden picture that we can only see when we hold it up to the light. And the light is Jesus! We have to believe and completely trust in Jesus in order to have the kingdom of God inside of us.

To take home: Ahead of time, use invisible ink to write a message (perhaps a scripture verse or their name) for each child to take home.

20

Never Fear, Jesus Is Here

You will need:
- a life preserver or a life jacket

Scripture: (Mark 4:35-41) *That evening, Jesus said to his followers, "Come with me across the lake." He and the followers left the people there. They went in the boat that Jesus was already sitting in. There were also other boats with them. A very strong wind came up on the lake. The waves began coming over the sides and into the boat. It was almost full of water. Jesus was at the back of the boat, sleeping with his head on a pillow. The followers went to him and woke him. They said, "Teacher, do you care about us? We will drown!" Jesus stood up and commanded the wind and the waves to stop. He said, "Quiet! Be still!" Then the wind stopped, and the lake became calm. Jesus said to his followers, "Why are you afraid? Do you still have no faith?" The followers were very afraid and asked each other, "What kind of man is this? Even the wind and the waves obey him!"*

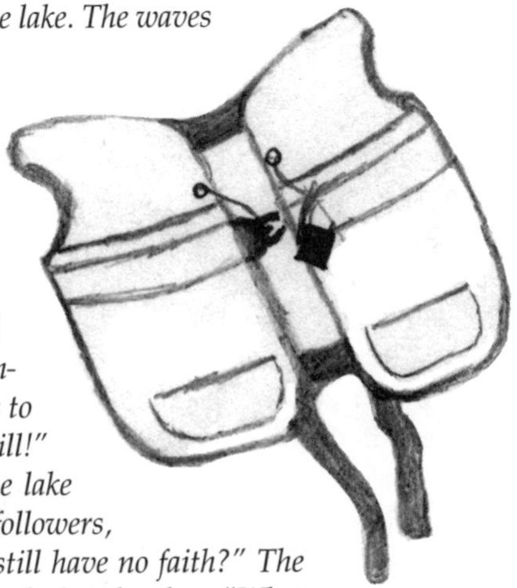

[Show the children the life preserver or life jacket.] What do I have here? Do you know what it is used for? That's right. We need it to keep safe when we go to a lake, are in a boat, or swim in deep water. Our Bible story today is about some people who were in

a boat, and they weren't wearing life jackets. Listen to the story from Mark 4. *[Read scripture.]*

Were the disciples doing what Jesus wanted them to do in this story? Yes, Jesus told them to come with him across the lake, so they got into the boat with Jesus. What bad thing happened to Jesus' followers in this story? Right; they got caught in the middle of the lake in a bad storm. Were they afraid? Yes, they thought they were going to drown. What did they do? They woke Jesus up. Remember, Jesus was asleep in the back of the boat. Evidently Jesus wasn't afraid, was he? Jesus told the wind and the waves to stop. And they did.

Sometimes bad things happen in our lives, don't they? Even when we are serving God and trying to do what God wants us to do, bad things can still happen. Does Jesus want us to be afraid when bad things happen? In our story, Jesus asked the disciples, "Why are you afraid? Do you still have no faith?" Jesus wants us to trust him completely when problems come in our lives. Here is what I want you children to always remember: No matter what bad things may be happening in our lives, when Jesus is in our boat, everything will be all right.

To take home: Give each child a piece of life-preserver-shaped candy. If you have used a life jacket instead to illustrate the story, you may have to explain that the candy is shaped like the life preservers used on some boats.

No Matter What

You will need:

- a large happy/sad face made from the pattern at the end of this sermon.

Scripture: (1 Thessalonians 5:16-18) *Always be happy. Never stop praying. Give thanks whatever happens. That is what God wants for you in Christ Jesus.*

[Show the children the large happy face and ask, "How is this person feeling?" When they say "happy," turn the face upside down to show the sad face and ask, "Are you sure?"]

Have you ever experienced happy/sad times in your life? You know—times when you are happy and sad at the same time? *[Invite one or two children to share a happy/sad experi-ence. If no one can think of one, the following illustration could be used.]* Birthdays can be happy/sad times. Long before your birthday, you count the months, weeks, and then days until your birthday. The big day finally arrives, and you have your party, open your presents, and blow out your candles. The day that took so long to get here goes by so quickly, and you may have a happy/sad feeling—happy that it's your birthday and you've had a great day, but sad that it's almost over.

[Read scripture.] Does this mean that when

something very sad happens we're supposed to pretend we are happy? If someone asks, "How are you doing?" should we put a big smile on our faces and say, "Everything's fine. Praise God!" even if we feel terrible inside? I don't think that's what God wants us to do. The Bible says we are to *give* thanks, not *feel* thankful. I believe we are to tell God—and sometimes others—our true feelings. God also wants us to give thanks even when we might feel sad or be going through a hard time. God is still a loving and awesome God, no matter what is happening in our lives. And we can praise God for the other blessings in our lives.

To take home: Make each child a happy/sad face cutout to take home to remind him or her to give thanks even in sad times.

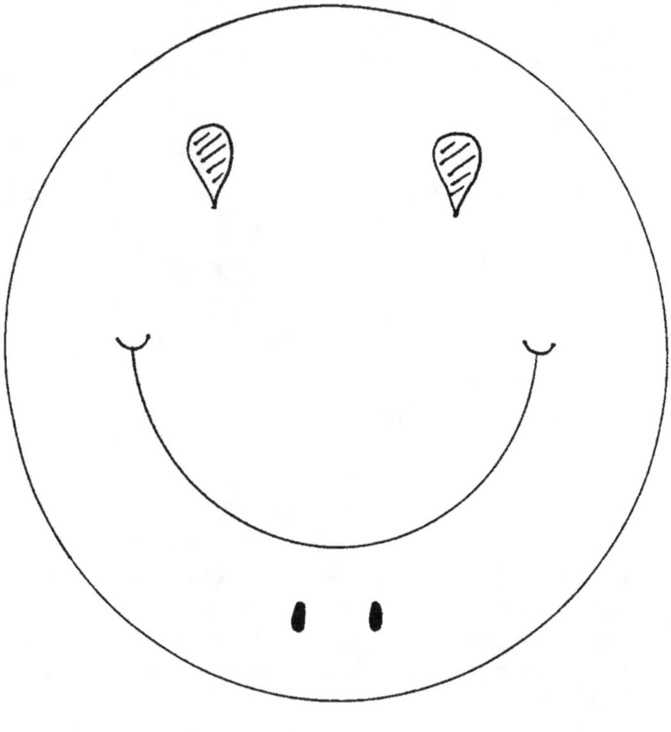

22

Noah and the Ark

You will need:

- a picture of Noah's ark or a toy representing the ark and Noah and the animals

Scripture: (Genesis 6:22) *Noah did everything that God commanded him.*

We've all probably heard the story of Noah's ark. What do you think we can learn from that story? Well, let's find out.

The world in Noah's day had become full of evil, and God decided that the world must be destroyed. But God looked at Noah and his family and saw that they loved God and tried to be obedient. So God told Noah to build an ark—a huge boat big enough to hold all of Noah's family and big enough to also hold two of every bird and animal, large and small, on the earth. That would take a big boat, wouldn't it?

Well, the Bible tells us that God told Noah exactly how to build the boat—what kind of wood to use, how big to make it. Noah did everything exactly as God said. And sure enough, when the boat was finished, it started to rain. It rained and rained and rained and rained! For forty days and forty nights, it kept raining. And soon, all the earth was covered with water, and everything was destroyed. But Noah and his family

and all the animals that came into the ark were safe and snug.

Now when Noah was building the ark, he could have said, "Oh, I don't think the boat needs to be quite as big as God said." What might have happened then? Maybe there wouldn't have been room for all the animals. Or maybe the ark would have sunk because the animals were too heavy. That was why it was so important for Noah to obey God's instructions exactly.

Do we sometimes forget to obey God exactly? I know I do. For instance, the Bible says I shouldn't say unkind things. But sometimes I think, "Oh well, it's only my husband I'm saying this unkind thing about." But God wants us to obey every single rule and to obey exactly, just the way Noah did. All of God's reasons for asking us to obey are perfect reasons because God is a perfect God. God knows what is best for us, and we will never be sorry for obeying God exactly.

To take home: Give each of the children a small box or package of animal crackers to remind them that we should obey God exactly, just as Noah did.

23

On the Level

You will need:

- a carpenter's level
- a small block of wood
- a ruler

Scripture: (Ecclesiastes 3:1) *There is a right time for everything. Everything on earth has its special season.*

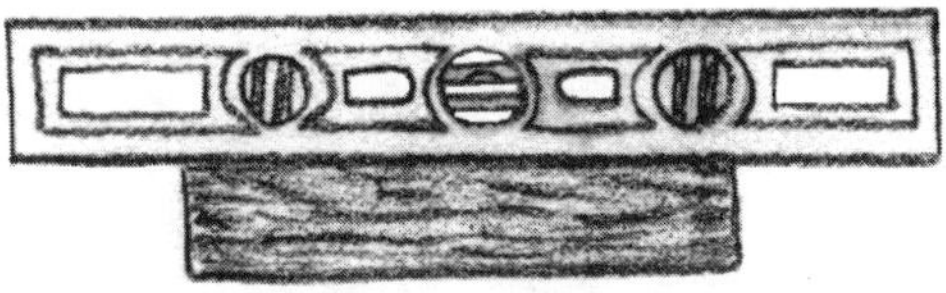

[Placing the ruler on the small block of wood (seesaw style), show the children how to use the carpenter's level to perfectly balance the ruler.] A carpenter uses a tool like this to make sure that what he or she is building is perfectly straight and in balance. It is important for our lives to have balance, also. God is the one who created us and knows what is best for us. But if we ask, we will be given wisdom and understanding to know how to find the right balance in all the parts of our lives.

God shows us how to find that perfect balance through the rules given to us in the Bible. For instance, the Bible tells us that we are to take one day out of our week to worship God and to rest. God knew we would need this special day of rest from our busy lives. So we are told in the Bible to remember to set this day aside for God.

God also knows that children need love and discipline in just the right balance. So parents, grandparents, teachers, and other adults are put in our lives to love us and to teach us right from wrong.

There are other places we need to find balance in our lives. For example, we know that too many sweets and not enough fruits and vegetables can make our bodies sick, don't we? It is important to find the right balance of healthy foods and sweets that will keep us healthy and strong.

We also know that too much work or play and not enough sleep will make us tired and cranky. If we are wise, we will find the right balance of the two.

Using God's wisdom to find just the right balance in everything we do will make us healthy in our bodies, in our minds, and in our spirits.

To take home: Give each child a small ruler as a reminder of the importance of using God's wisdom to find balance in our lives.

24

One in the Spirit

You will need: [If you do not use the take-home item, you will not need any materials to present this lesson.]

Scripture: (Ephesians 4:3, 4) *You are joined together with peace through the Spirit. Do all you can to continue together in this way. Let peace hold you together. There is one body and one Spirit. And God called you to have one hope.*

I'd like everyone to stand in front of me and please listen very carefully as we divide into groups. Ready? Will all those who are three or four years old stand over here. All those who are five or six years old stand here, and all those who are seven or older stand over there. Now, come back together, and we'll divide into groups again. This time, I'd like all those who are wearing white to stand over here, all those who are wearing blue stand over here, and all those who are wearing red or any other color to stand over here. Did you notice that the groups were different this time? All right, come back to the center, and we'll divide one more time. This time all those who have a dog stand over here, all those who have a cat stand right here, all those who have both a dog and a cat stand here, and all those who have no pets or some other kind of pet stand over there. Again, did you notice that our groups are different? Now, I'd like to ask all those of you who love Jesus to come and stand right here in front of me. Wow! Everyone stood up. Isn't it wonderful to know that even though we have many differences, we have one very important thing in common? We each love Jesus. And when we have Jesus in common, our differences don't really matter, do they?

Now if you are one of the younger children, you might not understand what it's like to be seven or ten. If you have a cat, you might not understand why John prefers dogs. Or if you have a dog, you might wonder what Jenny sees in cats. But we all share an understanding of what it means to love Jesus, and we want to please him. Sometimes it's easy to let our differences put us into little groups and keep us from enjoying friendships with those who might be different. But those differences are exactly what make us interesting to one another and help us learn something useful or new from one another. The things that make us different are what make us extra special to one another. Jesus intended for us to encourage each other when we're feeling sad or lonely and to enjoy each other's friendship. And the wonderful love we share for Jesus will always be something that can bring us together no matter what our differences are.

To take home: Before the children return to their seats, put an identical sticker (a cross or a picture of Jesus) on each child's hand. "I hope when you notice this sticker on one another's hands throughout the service and afterwards, that it will remind you that even though we are all different, the important thing is that we have Jesus in common."

25

Out on a Leash

You will need:

- a well-trained dog to demonstrate, if possible (or tell the story of training a dog)

Scripture: (Psalm 25:4, 5) *Lord, tell me your ways. Show me how to live. Guide me in your truth. Teach me, my God, my Savior. I trust you all day long.*

[Introduce the dog to the children. Consider taking the dog to the front before the children come forward so that those who are frightened of dogs may choose to remain in their seats.] I brought a special friend with me today to help with our lesson. Shep is a very smart and obedient dog. *[If the dog is cooperative, you might demonstrate some of its "tricks" at this point.]* Now Shep is a well-trained dog, but it took a long time for him to learn to obey. When Shep's owner first began working with him on a leash, Shep would sometimes see a squirrel on the ground and try to run ahead to chase the squirrel. Sometimes Shep would see something interesting in the grass along the road where they were walking, and then he would lag behind his owner. But once Shep learned how to obey his master, he knew that he was to walk just behind her, stopping when she stopped and

going ahead when his master said to go. Shep is much safer and happier when he follows his master's instructions.

You know, sometimes I think God's people act a bit like dogs on leashes. Sometimes, instead of asking what God wants us to do, we see something that we want and run ahead, chasing after it. Other times, we might know that God would like us to do something—maybe be kind to a friend, or help our grandma or grandpa with chores. But, instead of doing what we know we should, we lag behind. As we grow older, we should learn more and more about how to obey God. Just as Shep learned to listen to his master's voice, we should learn how to listen to God's voice that we hear in the Bible. We should learn to listen, obey, and follow—not running too far ahead, not lagging behind, but going exactly where God leads us because we know that God always wants the very best for us.

To take home: Reward the dog with a dog biscuit. Then give each child a dog-bone-shaped cookie. Cookie cutters in this shape are available from specialty stores and catalogs. Or you might be able to find dog-bone-shaped teething biscuits in the baby food section of your grocery store. "I hope these 'dog bones' will help you remember today's lesson."

26

Puppet Show

You will need:

- a hand puppet (give your puppet a name)

Scripture: (Acts 17:28*a*) *'We live in him. We walk in him. We are in him.'*

[Place the "empty" puppet across your lap.] I brought a puppet with me this morning. I call him JoJo. Would you like to meet him? *[Speaking to the puppet:]* Hey, JoJo! Say good morning to the boys and girls. JoJo? JoJo? Well, boys and girls, JoJo doesn't look very "alive" this morning, does he? Hey you! JoJo, are you awake this morning?

I'm sorry, children, I'm not having very good luck waking up JoJo. Do you have any ideas how we can get him moving this morning? *[If no one suggests putting your hand inside the puppet, guide the conversation in that direction.]* Oh, so you think maybe if I put my hand inside of the puppet, he'll snap to and "look alive"? Well, let's try that. *[Put a hand in the puppet and make him wave at the children, dance, and jump up and down.]*

Well, that's much better, isn't it? You know this reminds me a little bit of the way we are without God. The Bible says that it is only with God's help that we live and walk and exist at all. Of course God doesn't make us do anything. We aren't puppets, after all. But God is the one who gives us the strength to do all the things that we do. And God wants to lead us and guide us through the Holy Spirit to do things that will please God and help other people.

When we have God's Spirit in us, it brings us to life just as my hand brought this puppet to life. And with God's Spirit we can live our lives in a way that makes the Lord happy.

To take home: Give each child a simple hand puppet. These may be made by cutting two identical shapes from cloth or sturdy paper and gluing or sewing the halves together to form a puppet. (Gingerbread cookie cutters make good patterns but make sure the form is large enough for a child to fit his or her hand inside.) Or you could take old socks and draw faces on them to make puppets.

27

Ready for Battle

You will need:

- an umbrella
- a flashlight
- a bottle of vitamins
- a pair of shoes
- an army or other type of helmet
- a shield and sword (these may be made from cardboard)

Scripture: (Ephesians 6:10-17) *Finally, be strong in the Lord and in his great power. Wear the full armor of God. Wear God's armor so that you can fight against the devil's evil tricks. Our fight is not against people on earth. We are fighting against the rulers and authorities and the powers of this world's darkness. We are fighting against the spiritual powers of evil in the heavenly world. That is why you need to get God's full armor. Then on the day of evil you will be able to stand strong. And when you have finished the whole fight, you will still be standing. So stand strong, with the belt of truth tied around your waist. And on your chest wear the protection of right living. And on your feet wear the Good News of peace to help you stand strong. And also use the shield of faith. With that you can stop all the burning arrows of the Evil One. Accept God's salvation to be your helmet. And take the sword of the Spirit—that sword is the teaching of God.*

I brought some items with me this morning that help protect us from certain situations. The first item is an umbrella. Who can tell me what this protects us from? Yes, the rain, or possibly the sun. The second item is a flashlight. How can a flashlight help protect or keep us safe? If the electricity goes out in the night, we can use our flashlight to help us see so we won't bump into things and hurt ourselves. And what about this bottle of vitamins? We may take vitamins to help make our bodies strong so we can fight off sickness. The last thing I have is a pair of shoes. How many of you would like to walk through a sticker patch barefoot? Shoes help protect our feet from harmful objects.

Our scripture today talks about putting on the full armor of God so we can be protected. But it's not things like stickers or rain from which God's armor will protect us. The scripture says we need to wear God's armor in order to fight against the devil who tries to keep us from doing what God wants us to do. One of the pieces of armor that we need to put on is the helmet of salvation. Who wants to wear the helmet? We are saved through trusting in Jesus Christ as our Savior and Lord. We don't stand a chance against the devil if we don't ask Jesus to take away our sins and come into our heart. I also have a shield that one of us can hold. This represents the shield of faith. The Bible says that we can stop the burning arrows of the Evil One with the shield of faith. One more way we can win against the devil is with the sword of God's word. When Jesus was tempted by the devil in the wilderness, he spoke God's word to fight the devil. We need to learn what the Bible says so when the Evil One tries to tell us lies, we can fight him with God's truth.

To take home: Cut ten-to-twelve-inch circles of heavy-duty aluminum foil, which each child may mold into a helmet before going back to sit down.

Reflect the Light

You will need:

- a candle in a candlestick
- matches
- a handheld mirror

Scripture: (Ephesians 5:8-10) *In the past you were full of darkness, but now you are full of light in the Lord. So live like children who belong to the light. Light brings every kind of goodness, right living, and truth. Try to learn what pleases the Lord.*

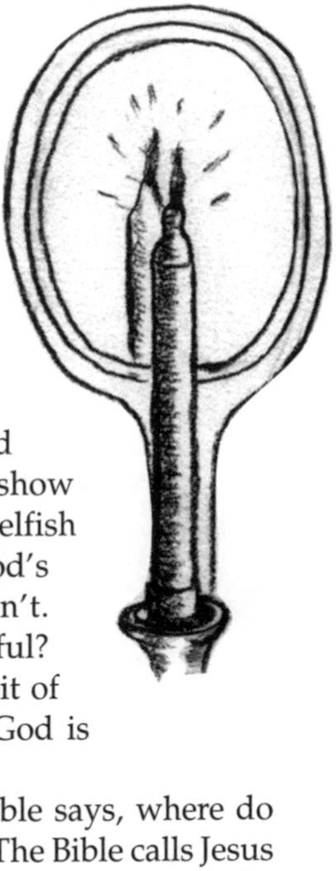

I have a candle with me today. Shall we light it? *[Carefully light the candle.]* In the book of Ephesians we are told that we Christians should live as children of light. What do you think that means? Let's read the scripture. *[Read scripture.]* It says here that if we are Christians, we are full of light from the Lord, and it also says that our behavior should show it. How can the way we act show God's light? If we act rude and selfish and mean, would that show God's light? No, it certainly wouldn't. What if we are kind and thoughtful? Would that show others a little bit of what God is like? Yes, because God is kind and thoughtful.

If we are full of light as the Bible says, where do you think that light comes from? The Bible calls Jesus the light of the world. Let's say that this candle stands for Jesus. I also have a mirror with me. We'll say that the mirror stands for you. If I hold the mirror close to the candle, what happens? That's right, we see a reflection of the candle, don't we? The reflection of the candlelight in the mirror seems to make the candlelight even brighter. This is how it is in our lives. If we stay close to Jesus and obey his Word, our lives will reflect his light, and people will be able to see a little bit of Jesus' light by watching us. If we all would reflect the light of Jesus in the way we act and the way we talk, then the world would see how good and wonderful God is!

To take home: Give each child a small pocket-size mirror to remind him or her that we are to reflect the light of Jesus in all that we do. You may pass out the mirrors and ask the children to try to catch the reflection of the candle in their mirrors. "See how bright the light is when we are all trying to reflect the true light? Let's remember that this is just the way it is with Jesus' light."

29

Riddle Me That

You will need:
- a book of riddles

Scripture: (Matthew 22:23-40) [The scripture is told in story form.]

[Read several riddles from the book and see if the children can guess the answers.] This kind of a joke is called a riddle. Riddles can be pretty tricky, can't they?

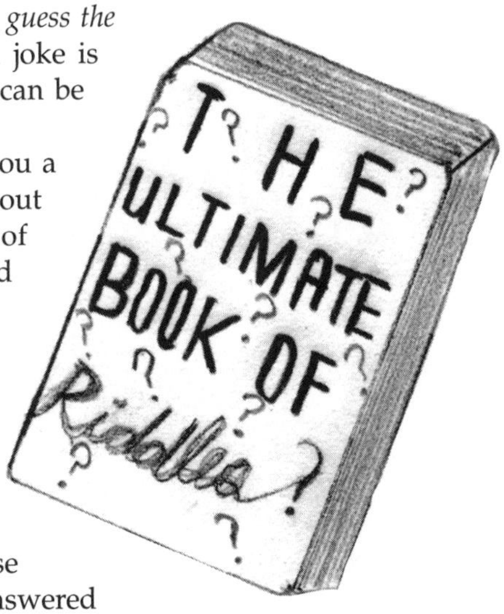

Today I want to tell you a story from the Bible about two different groups of people who each asked Jesus a question to try to trick him.

The first group to ask Jesus a question was the Sadducees. These people didn't believe that those who had died would rise from the dead. Jesus answered their question, and the Bible says it was such a good answer that they were amazed at Jesus' teaching. They thought, "Wow! This guy is good! He gave a really good answer to a really tough question."

The second group of people to ask Jesus a question was the Pharisees. Now the Pharisees believed differently from the Sadducees. It was as if they were on different teams. The Pharisees heard that Jesus' answer to the Sadducees' question had left them speechless, so they may have thought, "Well, Jesus might be able to stump those Sadducees, but we're too smart for that. We've got a really good question—one he surely won't be able to answer." This is what they asked Jesus: "What is the greatest commandment in the law?" Now they weren't just talking about the Ten Commandments. The rabbis (or teachers) in Jesus' day had counted 613 different rules that God had given. So they were asking Jesus to pick which commandment was the most important out of 613.

Do you know what Jesus said? Jesus answered, "Love the Lord your God with all your heart, soul and mind." And he even gave them a bonus answer. He said, "And the second commandment is like the first: 'Love your neighbor as you love yourself.'" Jesus was not tricked, and his answers gave us two very important commandments to live by.

To take home: Copy riddles from the book onto three-by-five-inch index cards and give a different one to each child.

30

Scattered to the Wind

You will need:

- a handful of light, downy feathers (a feather pillow is a good source for these)

Scripture: (Proverbs 16:28) *An evil person causes trouble. And a person who gossips ruins friendships.*

I brought some feathers with me today. These were sewn tightly into a feather pillow, but I took them out to make a point that I hope will help us understand today's scripture. *[Read scripture.]* I'm going to have each of you take a handful of these feathers. Now I want you to stand up and blow as hard as you can to scatter your feathers out into the congregation. *[When the children have scattered the feathers, ask them to sit down again.]*

Remember that our scripture was about troublemakers and gossips. We know what a troublemaker is, don't we? That's right. It's someone who makes trouble. But what is a gossip? Does anyone know what the word "gossip" means? Well, gossip is when we tell stories that aren't very nice about other people. The stories might be true or might even be lies. But whichever they are, the Bible says that Christians should not have any part in gossiping.

When I was little, my mother always said that if you can't say something nice about someone, you shouldn't say anything at all. And I think that's what this verse in the Bible is also saying.

Now, what if I asked you to go out into the congregation and pick up all the feathers you scattered? It would take a long time, wouldn't it? In fact, it would be almost impossible to find every one of them because they scattered so far. Some of them might have stuck in someone's clothes or hair and will get carried out of the church. Some of the feathers are probably hiding under the pews, and you won't see them until a breeze blows them up again or the janitor sweeps them up. You see, gossip is just like these feathers. When we tell unkind stories about people, those stories usually get spread to another person and another and another. And before long, it's impossible to take back our unkind words because they've traveled so far. We don't want to be troublemakers or hurt our friends with unkind words. I hope these feathers will remind us how hard it is to take back words of gossip. Let's remember that it would be far better not say them in the first place.

To take home: Give each child a larger feather to take home. These may be purchased at craft stores, or you may select some of the larger feathers found in a feather pillow.

Note: Be sure you check with your church janitor or plan to clean the feathers up yourself after the service—especially if your church has two or more services!

31

See for Yourself

You will need:

- a teenage or adult volunteer
- chewy, fruit-flavored candy

Scripture: (Acts 20:21, 24) *I warned both Jews and Greeks to change their lives and turn to God. And I told them all to believe in our Lord Jesus. I don't care about my own life. The most important thing is that I complete my mission. I want to finish the work that the Lord Jesus gave me—to tell people the Good News about God's grace.*

[The conversation between you and the volunteer should go like this:]

You: Hi there. Look what I have. *[Hold up a piece of the candy.]* It's my favorite kind of candy in the whole world. It comes in all kinds of wonderful fruity flavors. Orange is my favorite. Before you even put it into your mouth, your mouth starts to water just waiting for that tangy, fruity burst of flavor. Then when you do taste it, *[put one in your mouth]* your mouth just comes alive. It's chewy at first. Then it just melts in your mouth. Isn't it just the best thing you've ever tasted?

Volunteer: Well, I don't really know . . .

You: What do you mean you don't know? I just described in detail how it tasted.

Volunteer: Yes, you did, and I have a little idea of what it might taste like. But would it be asking too much for me to try one myself?

You: Hey, what a great idea! Why didn't I think of that?

Volunteer: *[Eats a candy.]* Hey! You're right. This is wonderful, just like you said. *[Continues to gush over how good it is as he or she finishes the candy.]* Maybe the children would like to try one, too.

You: You're just full of good ideas today.

[Give each child a piece of candy. Continue the sermon as they enjoy their candy.] You know, we can tell people about our friendship with Christ. We can tell them how Jesus set us free from sin, how he is always there for us, how we can have wonderful fellowship with him through prayer, and how he fills that empty feeling that we once had. But just like *(volunteer's name)* here didn't know what the candy tasted like until he or she actually ate one, others cannot experience Christ until they have asked Christ to come into their hearts and lives. The apostle Paul said that he didn't care about his own life. *[Read scripture.]* The most important thing to Paul was to tell people about Jesus so they could experience Jesus for themselves.

To take home: Give each child another piece of candy to take home or share with someone else.

Shhh! Don't Tell

You will need: [If you do not use the take-home item, you will not need any materials to present this lesson.]

Scripture: (Matthew 6:1-4) *"Be careful! When you do good things, don't do them in front of people to be seen by them. If you do that, then you will have no reward from your Father in heaven. When you give to the poor, don't be like the hypocrites. They blow trumpets before they give so that people will see them. They do that in the synagogues and on the streets. They want other people to honor them. I tell you the truth. Those hypocrites already have their full reward. So when you give to the poor, give very secretly. Don't let anyone know what you are doing. Your giving should be done in secret. Your Father can see what is done in secret, and he will reward you."*

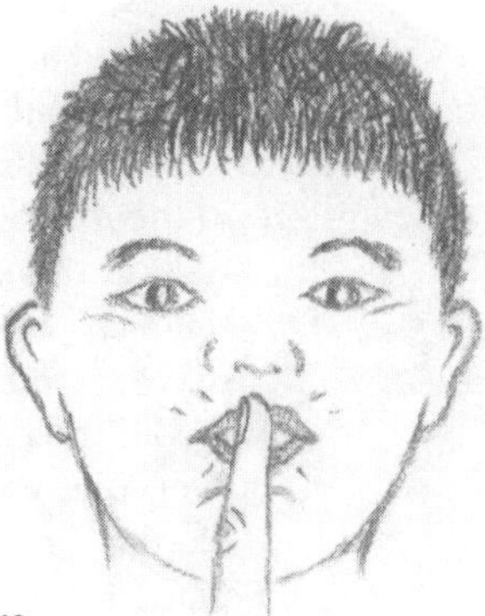

I have a story to tell you about two men. The first man's name was Mr. Smith. He was an elderly man who never married. He lived a simple life but had always been a hard worker and saved quite a sum of money. One day as he was walking to the local restaurant to eat his supper, he passed the boys' and girls' club where children came after school to play or do their homework until their parents came to pick them up. He had walked by the club many times, but for some reason that evening he stopped and peered in the window. He saw children shooting baskets, jumping rope, playing board games, and doing their homework. He noticed that one of the backboards was broken and many pieces of tile were missing from the floor. Only half of the lights worked, and there weren't enough tables for the children who were doing schoolwork. As the man ate his supper that evening he thought about the children and decided he would devote his life's savings to improving the club. After supper, he told his plans to the director of the girls' and boys' club, who nearly fell over backwards! The only condition, the elderly man said, was that no one could know where the money had come from. And no one ever did.

In a city not too far away lived another man, Mr. Roble. He was also quite wealthy, and he wanted people to know it. He had a very nice home with a swimming pool, three expensive cars, and a fancy camper. One day as he was having coffee with his friends, as he always did, the subject of the city park came up. It was in very bad condition. The playground equipment was old and falling apart. There were weeds where flower gardens should have been, and the beautiful fountain in the middle of the park, where water once cascaded gracefully, held only dead leaves. The man declared right then and there to his friends that he planned to give the money to repair the park. Right after his coffee break, he went straight to the mayor and told him of his plans. But he said, "I will do this on the condition that the park will be just the way I want it." So he had new flower gardens planted and the beautiful fountain rebuilt with a statue of himself right in the middle. A large sign greeted everyone who entered. *Welcome to Roble Park,* it said. On each piece of new playground equipment was a plaque that read: *In honor of the honorable, most noble Mr. Roble.* The man was quite proud of himself, and he loved to tell of the wonderful things he had done. *[Read scripture and explain the take-home item.]*

To take home: Give each child a folded piece of paper on which you have written a good deed that he or she can do secretly sometime during the week. Examples: *Load the dishwasher without being told. Write a note thanking your parents for all that they do for you. Pick up litter in your neighborhood, and so on.*

33

Some Dandy Lions

You will need:

- a blossom from a dandelion weed for each child (these are less messy when they are in the yellow flower stage)

Scripture: (Daniel 6:1-23) [The scripture is told in story form.]

The Bible tells the story of a young man named Daniel. Now Daniel loved God, and it showed in the way he lived his life. He was faithful and honest and always very responsible. Because of these great qualities, the king gave Daniel a very important job—the job of being the boss over 120 princes of the land! But the princes didn't like having a boss, and they started looking for a way to get rid of Daniel. When they noticed that Daniel was always faithful in praying to God three times every day, they saw their chance. They convinced the king to make a new law that declared that all the people should pray only to the king—not to God. And to make matters worse, they made a rule that if anyone *did* pray to God, the punishment would be imprisonment in a den of hungry lions!

Well, Daniel knew that it would be very wrong to pray to anyone except God. So he went right up to his room and knelt down in front of his open windows to pray and give thanks to God, just like he always had. But some of the rulers saw Daniel praying to God—which was just what they'd wanted all along—and they ran back to the king and tattled on Daniel.

"Didn't you make a law that anyone who prays to someone other than Your Majesty for the next thirty days would be thrown into the lions' den?" they asked.

"Why, yes," the king replied; "I did." Then they told him about Daniel. Now, the king liked Daniel, and he didn't want to throw him to the lions, but he had signed a law that couldn't be broken. So in the end, he was forced to throw Daniel in with those hungry lions. When he did, he told Daniel, "May the God you worship rescue you!" And sure enough, the next morning when he went to the lions' den, expecting to see that Daniel had been eaten by the lions, he saw Daniel standing there without one scratch on him! Because Daniel trusted God, God shut the lions' mouths and saved Daniel! I bet Daniel thought it was pretty "dandy" of those lions not to eat him, don't you? And whenever we're in danger, we can trust God to take care of us just the way he took care of Daniel.

To take home: Give each child a dandelion as a reminder of how God watched over Daniel in the lions' den.

Soup's On

You will need:

- labels from cans of vegetables or pictures of vegetables cut from grocery ads or magazines (put each of these in a separate paper bag)
- a picture of a roast
- a large pot
- a pitcher
- a wooden spoon

Scripture: (Hebrews 13:16) *Do not forget to do good to others. And share with them what you have. These are the sacrifices that please God.*

[Distribute paper bags to the children and ask them not to open them yet.] How many of us like to pretend? God gave us such wonderful imaginations, and pretending is a great way to use our imaginations. Today we are going to pretend that we are making soup. I bought this roast at the grocery store so first I'm going to cut it up and let it boil for a while. *[Hold up the picture of the roast and begin to tear it into pieces and put it in the pot. Pretend to pour water from the pitcher into the pot.]* I have to be sure to stir it from time to time. I think our soup is missing some ingredients. What about the vegetables? Does anyone have any vegetables to add to our soup? Look in your paper bags now and see what you find. Vegetables? Great! *[Ask each child to come up*

one by one to drop the vegetables into the pot. Keep stirring the soup.] This is going to be wonderful soup. Would you like to try some? Hold out your bowls, and I'll give you some. *[Cup your hands to show the children how to make a "bowl."]* Mmmm, isn't this delicious? If we had kept all the ingredients to ourselves, we would have missed out on this treat. I want to read you our Bible verse from Hebrews 13. *[Read scripture.]*

To take home: Give each child a can of vegetables to share with someone this week or have the children place the cans where food items are being collected.

Note: This sermon can be used on a Sunday that your church is collecting food for the needy.

35

Sow the Word

You will need:

- an apple
- a knife

Scripture: (Luke 8:4-15) [The scripture is told in story form.]

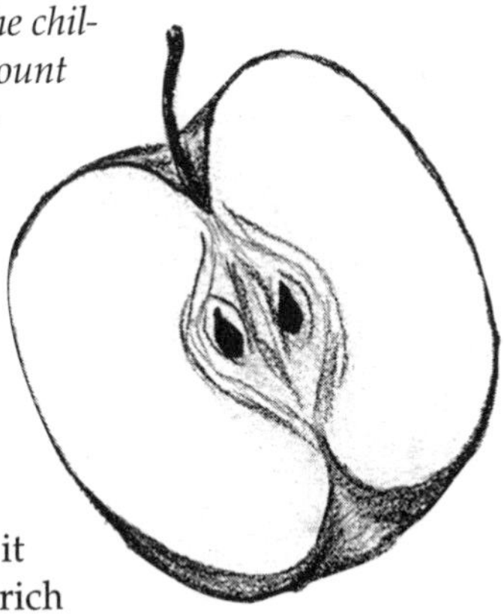

[Cut the apple in half and show the children the seeds. Ask the children to count the seeds with you.] There is a saying that goes, "Anyone can tell how many seeds are in an apple; only God can tell how many apples are in a seed." What do you think this means? What would happen if I planted one of these seeds in the ground and watered it? If it got just what it needed—sunshine, water, and rich soil—it would grow into an apple tree, wouldn't it? And after several years it would begin to grow apples. We wouldn't know how many apples that tree would produce in its lifetime, but we can guess it would be a lot. And to think it started from one tiny seed.

Jesus told a story about a farmer and his seed. He tells about a seed that fell by the road, a seed that fell on rocky ground, and a seed that fell among thorny weeds. None of the seeds grew to be a healthy plant. But the last seed Jesus told about was seed that fell on good ground, and it grew into many healthy plants that made one hundred times more than what was planted. Jesus told this story to teach a lesson.

He said the seed that fell on good ground "is like those who hear God's teaching with a good, honest heart. They obey God's teaching and patiently produce good fruit." *[Hold up an apple seed.]* God's word is like this seed. We can "plant" the seed by sharing the good news of Jesus Christ with other people, by living a life of love and service to God so that other people will want what we have, and by pointing them to Jesus. As Christians, we need to plant seed, or to share God's word, wherever we go because, just as only God knows how many apples will grow from this seed, only God knows how many people will come into the kingdom because we have shared God's word.

To take home: Give each child an apple-shaped magnet or sticker to take home. "I hope that when you see this magnet (or sticker) on your refrigerator at home, it will remind you that by sharing the good news of Jesus with others, you are planting seeds that might help others know Jesus, too."

36

String Me Along

You will need:

- a large, colorful balloon filled with helium and tied to a long string

Scripture: (Psalm 121:7) *The Lord will guard you from all dangers. He will guard your life.*

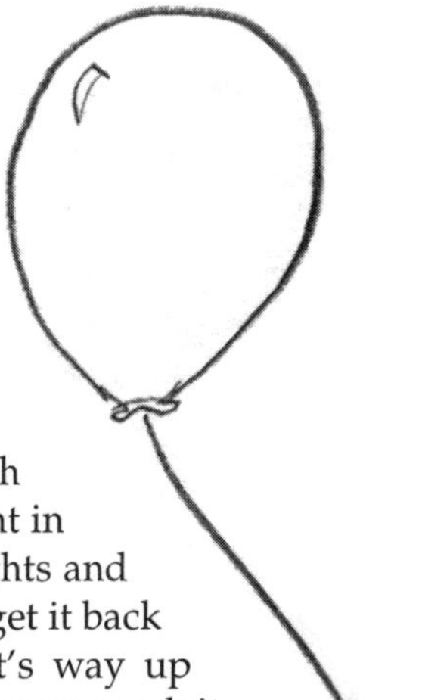

[As the children come to the front of the church, hold the balloon in your lap. When they have all gathered around, gradually release the string and allow the balloon to float to the ceiling, keeping a tight hold on the string. The higher it can go, the more impressive.]

Wow! Do you see how high my balloon is going? If it goes much higher, I'm afraid it might get caught in the fans or bump into one of the lights and pop. Can anyone reach up there to get it back down here where it's safe? No? It's way up there, isn't it? I'm not sure we could even reach it with a long ladder. Well, how could we get it down? *[Ask the children for some ideas.]* Oh, so you think if we just pull on this string we can bring it back down where it's safe? Well, let's try that.

You know, this reminds me of when I was a little child. I became separated from my parents in a crowd of people at the state fair. *[Tell your own story of being lost as a child.]* Have you ever been lost or separated from your parents for a short time? It's a pretty scary feeling, isn't it? At times such as this, it might feel as though you are by yourself with no one watching over you. You might feel a little bit like that balloon, alone and surrounded by danger. When that happened to me, my heart was beating like a drum and I was just about to start crying when I spotted my parents. They were just ahead of me in the crowd, and they had been watching over me, making sure I was safe all along.

Sometimes even grown-ups feel alone and scared. But we need to remember that we are never really alone. We are kind of like this balloon on a string. Even though we might feel that we're alone and floating out of control, God's warm, protecting hand is on our string, ready to pull us back to safety whenever we are in trouble or in need of help or guidance. All we have to do is ask!

To take home: Give each child a helium-filled balloon on a string to take home. You might want to wait to hand these to the children as they leave the sanctuary.

Suffering— A Good Thing?

You will need:
- one-half to one yard of fabric
- a finished quilt
- a needle and thread
- a pair of sewing scissors

Scripture: (Hebrews 2:10*b*) *So God made perfect the One who leads people to salvation. He made Jesus a perfect Savior through Jesus' suffering.*

(Hebrews 5:8) *Even though Jesus was the Son of God, he learned to obey by what he suffered.*

Who knows what the word "suffer" means? Sometimes it is defined as wanting what you don't have or having what you don't want. When we were having weeks of weather with temperatures over one hundred degrees this summer, you might have heard someone say that he or she was suffering from the heat, or wanting something he or she didn't have—cool weather. If you have a cold, you might say that you're suffering from a cold. You have something you don't want—a runny nose, sore throat, coughing, and everything else that goes with

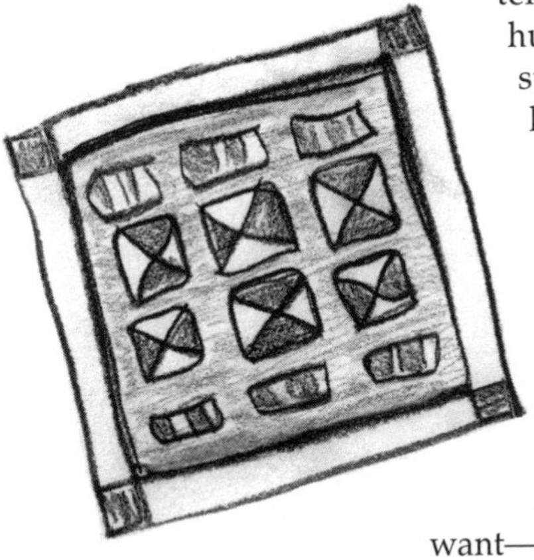

a cold. How many of you like to suffer? Don't everyone raise your hands at once! We often wish that we would never have any more trouble or hurt in our lives, don't we?

The Bible has some things to say about suffering. For one thing, it tells us that Jesus suffered. Listen to these two verses in Hebrews. *[Read scriptures.]*

Let me see if I can help you understand all of this a little better. I have a piece of fabric here. It's a nice piece of fabric. See, it doesn't have any holes or tears in it, and it's bright and pretty, isn't it? This could represent our lives. We might think our lives are just fine and pretty the way they are. Then something happens that hurts us. *[Make a cut in the fabric.]* We can call this suffering. And we don't understand why our lives, which we thought were going just fine the way they were, have to be different in a way that we don't like. *[Take a needle and sew some stitches in the fabric.]* Then, some more hurtful things happen, like this needle going through the fabric. Ouch! We wonder why God, who loves us so much, is allowing this to happen to us. Let's look back to the reasons that Jesus had to suffer. Can you remember what the scripture said? The Bible says that, through suffering, Jesus: (1) was made perfect and (2) learned to obey God. Through suffering, we may also learn to obey God and become more like Jesus. Through suffering, we can become people who are more useful and beautiful for Christ's sake, *[hold up the quilt]* just like this quilt that has been cut and sewn. It is much more beautiful and useful than the plain pieces of fabric it was made from, isn't it?

To take home: Give each child a colorful square of fabric to take home as a reminder that, even though we don't enjoy it, suffering can be good when it makes us more like Jesus.

38

The Greatest Is Love

You will need:

- wooden craftsticks on which you have written various spiritual gifts: *prophecy, knowledge, faith, discernment, giving, ser-vice, wisdom, leadership, teaching, healing, encouragement, miracle working*
- a ribbon approximately ten inches long, on which the word "love" is written

Scripture: (Colossians 3:14 CEV) *Love is more important than anything else. It is what ties everything completely together.*

The Bible talks about the gifts that God gives to people. On each of these sticks I've written the name of a different gift that the Bible tells about. *[As you hand these out, read them to the children and maybe explain just a little about a few of the gifts.]* All of these gifts are good, but there is something even more important than any of these gifts. Listen carefully to the Bible verse to see if you can figure out what it is. *[Read scripture.]*

I have a ribbon that I've written the answer on. Can anyone read it? It says "love." And love is the thing that is more important than any of the gifts God gives us. I would like for each of you to hand me your stick, and I will tie this ribbon around the sticks. If we are using our gifts with love for God and for one another, then love holds those gifts and our lives together. But if we don't have love *[untie ribbon and let the sticks fall to the ground]* everything just falls apart. It is only when we yield our lives to God, who is love, and ask God to fill us with the Holy Spirit that we can truly love.

To take home: Let each child take home a craftstick on which you have written the word "love" and decorated with markers.

39

The Truth Helps

You will need:

- three candy kisses (remove the candy from the wrapper and replace with wads of foil which you have molded into "kiss" shapes)

Scripture: (Proverbs 27:6) *The slap of a friend can be trusted to help you. But the kisses of an enemy are nothing but lies.*

[Ask a child to hold out his or her hand. Show the candy kisses that you have replaced with wads of foil.] If I gave you a choice, which would you rather have? A slap on the hand or these candy kisses? Oh, you chose the kisses? I thought you would. Well, go ahead and open one of your kisses. What's inside? Just an old hunk of foil? Open another one. Same thing? Ha! I "foiled" you, didn't I?

[Read scripture.] What do you think this verse means? At times our friends may tell us things about ourselves we don't like hearing. They may say something such as, "I don't think you should cheat on your test," or "You were rude to your mom. I think you should apologize." An enemy will tell us anything we want to hear, even if it's a lie. The words of an enemy will look good at first, just as these kisses did, but in the end their lies will hurt us, just as these wads of foil would if we tried to eat them.

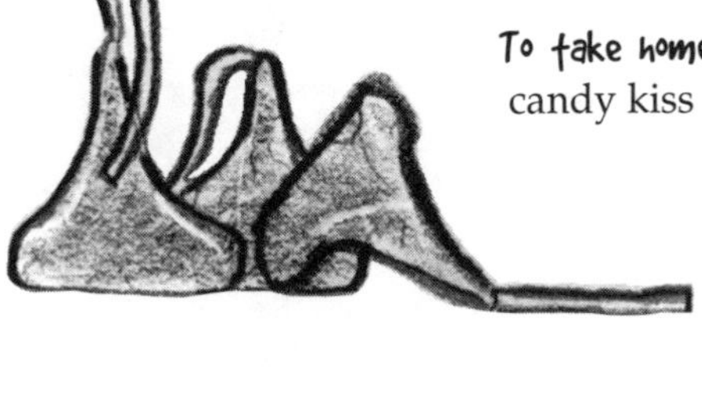

To take home: Give each child a real candy kiss to take home.

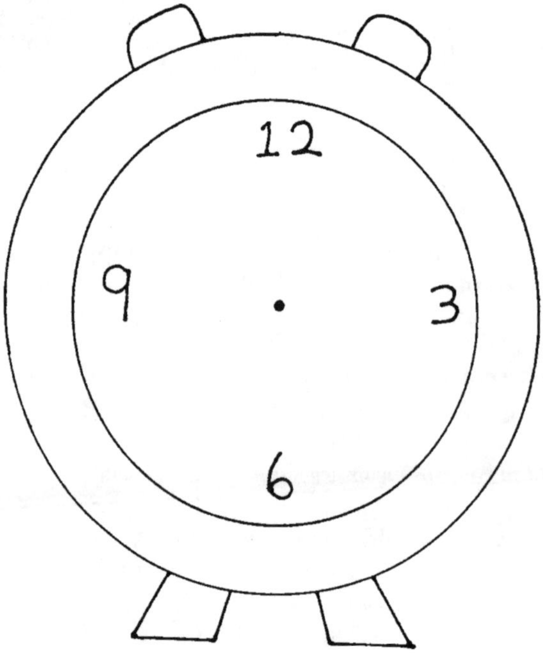

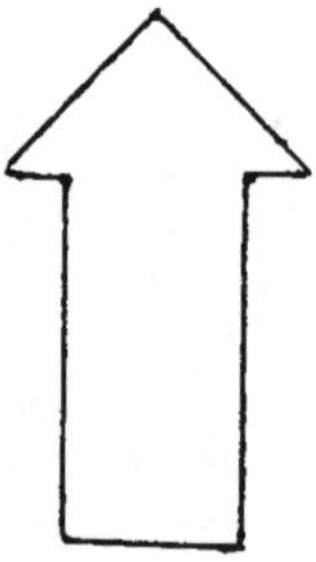

- *Cut two.*
- *Make one slightly shorter than the other.*

40

Thief in the Night

You will need:

- three or four coffee cans or similar containers
- several pennies or buttons for each child
- an alarm clock

Scripture: (2 Peter 3:10*a*, 11*b*-14) *But the day the Lord comes again will be a surprise, like a thief. . . . So what kind of people should you be? You should live holy lives and serve God. You should wait for the day of God and look forward to its coming. When that day comes, the skies will be destroyed with fire, and everything in the skies will melt with heat. But God made a promise to us. And we are waiting for what he promised—a new heaven and a new earth where goodness lives. Dear friends, we are waiting for this to happen. So try as hard as you can to be without sin and without fault. Try to be at peace with God.*

[Right before going up to give the children's message, set the alarm clock to go off in approximately three minutes, but keep the clock hidden.] We're going to have some fun playing a game this morning. I've brought some coffee cans with me, and I'm going to set them out here. Each of you will have several pennies, and

the object of the game is to toss the pennies and try to get them to land in one of the cans. *[The alarm clock should go off just as the children are beginning to have fun with the game.]* Okay. This game is over. Everyone needs to stop playing right now and come over here. I have something very important to tell you. It's a promise that the Lord gave us. The Bible says that Jesus is going to come back to earth again. No one knows when this will happen. It could be tomorrow; it could be ten years or a hundred years from now.

In the third chapter of 2 Peter we read that the day the Lord comes again will be a surprise. Were we surprised when this alarm clock went off? When Jesus comes again, it will be like that. We will be going about our everyday activities and then—surprise!—Jesus will appear. What should we be doing when Jesus comes back? Peter asks, "So what kind of people should you be?" He answers his own question by saying, "You should live holy lives and serve God. You should wait for the day of God and look forward to its coming. So try as hard as you can to be without sin and without fault. Try to be at peace with God." It is very important for us to live in a way that will please Jesus and give glory to God. That way, the day Jesus returns to earth will be a wonderful surprise, not an unwelcome one.

To take home: Make alarm clocks for each child using the pattern that appears on page 88. Use metal fasteners to attach the hands to the clock.

41

Three in One

You will need:

- a pitcher of water
- a block of ice that has been made with water poured from the pitcher
- a container of hot water which has been boiled using water poured from the pitcher

Scripture: (2 Corinthians 13:14) *The grace of the Lord Jesus Christ, the love of God, and the fellowship of the Holy Spirit be with you all.*

Have you ever heard the word "Trinity"? It's a big word, isn't it? This means that God is known in three ways. One way is God, the Father. Another way is God, the Son, or Jesus. And the third way is God, the Holy Spirit. So we have the Father, the Son, and the Holy Spirit. We call this the Holy Trinity. Yet over and over, the Bible says that there is only one God. How can this be?

The Trinity is a mystery too deep to understand fully and one that we have to accept by faith. One way that can help us understand the Trinity a little better is with the use of an illustration. Last night I filled this pitcher with water. From this pitcher, I poured some of the water into a pan and boiled it on the stove this morning. Then I poured the boiling water into this container. If everyone will stand away from the container I'll open it, and we will see what happens to the water when it is heated. *[Carefully open the container and show the children the steam that rises. Don't forget to close the lid tightly and put the container out of reach before moving on.]* Now, I also poured some of the water into another container and put it in the freezer. When I opened the freezer this morning, the water had turned into this solid block of ice.

Do you see that the very same water from this pitcher has three different forms? It can be liquid, as it is in the pitcher; it can be steam, as it is when it is heated; or it can be solid, as it is when it is frozen. The water has three very different qualities, yet it is all the same water. This is similar to what we mean when we say that God is three in one. We will probably never completely understand the Trinity, but maybe this will help us understand just a little better.

To take home: Give each child an ice cube in a small paper cup.

Note: This sermon is appropriate anytime, but especially on Trinity Sunday.

42

Tug-of-War

You will need:

- a garden tool for digging up dandelions
- a dandelion root, if dandelions are in season *(optional)*

Scripture: (Galatians 5:16, 17, 24, 25) *So I tell you: Live by following the Spirit. Then you will not do what your sinful selves want. Our sinful selves want what is against the Spirit. The Spirit wants what is against our sinful selves. The two are against each other. So you must not do just what you please. Those who belong to Christ Jesus have crucified their own sinful selves. They have given up their old selfish feelings and the evil things they wanted to do. We get our new life from the Spirit. So we should follow the Spirit.*

I brought a special tool with me this morning. Does anyone know what this is used for? This is a garden tool that is used to dig up dandelions. You put it in the ground, turn it, and the dandelion comes up, root and all. When you're digging dandelions, it's important to get the whole root. If you just cut off its head or the flower, it may look as though you've gotten rid of the weed, but soon another one will grow.

That reminds me of sin in our lives. We are all born sinners. Galatians 5:17 says that without God's spirit in our lives we want to do things that don't make God happy. God's spirit wants us to do what is right—what is against our sinful selves. The two—God's spirit and our sinful selves—are against each other. But we must have God's Spirit within us to win this battle and stop doing what we please. Sometimes we may do bad things that we don't really like doing, such as lying, cheating, or fighting with our brothers or sisters. We can try and try to quit doing these things on our own, but it will be just like pulling the head off the dandelion. Soon we will again do the very things we don't want to do!

Paul goes on to tell us in Galatians 5 that those who belong to Christ Jesus have put their sinful selves to death. They have given up their old selfish feelings and the bad things they wanted to do. The Bible tells us: "We get our new life from the Spirit. So we should follow the Spirit." When we give our lives to Jesus, we then have the power to stop sinning, just as using this tool helps get the whole dandelion, root and all. When we belong to Jesus, God's Spirit comes into our lives and helps us not do the bad things we don't want to do and start doing the good things that we do want to do.

To take home: Use a photocopier to enlarge the picture of the dandelion on the previous page, and give each child a copy to take home and color. You may wish to copy part of the scripture onto the page, also.

43

White as Snow

You will need: [If you do not use the take-home item, you will not need any materials to present this lesson.]

Scripture: (Isaiah 1:18*b*) *"Your sins are red like deep red cloth. But they can be as white as snow. Your sins are bright red. But you can be white like wool."*

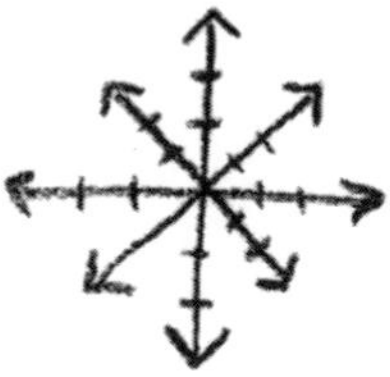

I want you to use your imagination with me. Imagine that we are walking down a road and we come to a place where the road forks off in two directions. Down one fork, the pathway is smooth and clean with only a few bumps and cracks in the road. Down the other fork, we see that the path is littered with trash and weeds and deep cracks. Sometimes it seems as if our lives are like this. Some of us seem to get along pretty well. Our lives are more like the clean, smooth pathway. We don't get into trouble very often and when we do, it's nothing too serious. Others of us are more like the bumpy, messy path. As much as we may not like it, we seem to do naughty things and get into trouble all the time.

Now, let's use our imaginations again. Picture that fork in the road again with one clean pathway and one rough, dirty pathway. Now imagine that it begins to snow. The snowflakes fall and fall and fall, and soon both of the pathways are covered with several inches of snow. Now when we look down the road in either direction we can't tell a difference between the two. Both of the pathways look smooth and clean and new.

Did you know that the Bible tells us that Jesus can make our lives just like those pathways? If we've only done a few bad things in our lives, we still need Jesus to forgive us and make our lives clean and new. And even if we've done many bad things, when we ask Jesus to forgive us, he promises that he will wash our sins away and make us just as clean as if we'd never done one bad thing! Isn't it wonderful to know that Jesus can make us clean again, no matter how bad we've acted?

To take home: Cut out snowflakes from white paper and give one to each child. Tell the children, "When you look at this 'snowflake,' I hope you will remember that no matter how good or bad we've been, we need Jesus to wash our sins away and make us white as snow."

44

Willing Workers

You will need:

- a dishrag, feather duster, scrub brush, schoolbook, and other props to represent housework and homework

Scripture: (Colossians 3:23) *In all the work you are doing, work the best you can. Work as if you were working for the Lord, not for men.*

I have a story I'd like to tell you. It's a story about a girl who had four brothers and two sisters. With such a large family, you can imagine that there were lots of dishes to wash after mealtimes. At the time, most people didn't have dishwashers, so everyone had to pitch in and do his or her part. At first, this girl's job was to take the leftover food scraps out to the cats, and then she was to come back in and help with another job. But do you know what? It would take this little girl the longest time to give the cats the scraps—so long, in fact, that most of the time when she got back inside, the dishes were already washed.

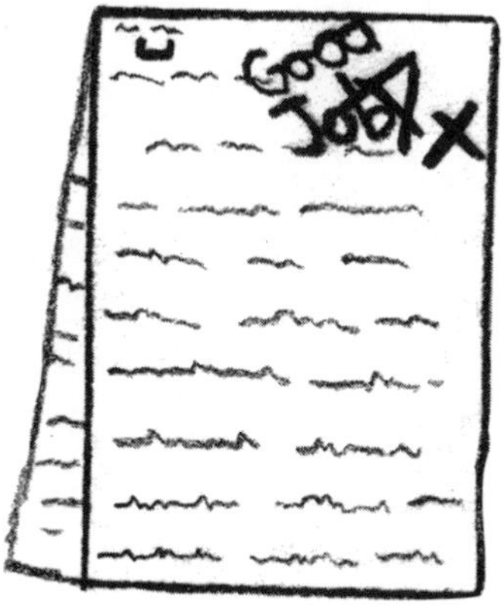

Well, her family soon caught on to her taking-out-the-scraps trick, so they assigned that job to someone else. When the girl got her new assignment, it just so happened that she had to go to the bathroom badly and couldn't wait. You can guess that she was in the bathroom a really long time. Sometimes she would even crawl out of the bathroom window.

Surely none of us has ever done anything like that! In truth, I'm afraid all of us have probably tried to get out of a job we didn't like at some time or another in our lives.

I'd like to read a verse in the Bible that talks about work. *[Read scripture.]* If we are students, we should do the best we can in school. If our moms or dads ask us to do a job at home, instead of doing a sloppy, half-done job, we should do the best that we can do. And in church, we should also do our best at the jobs that we agree to do. As the scripture says, we should work as if we are working for the Lord, not for other people—as if Jesus was our boss.

To take home: Using permanent markers, write the scripture reference on rectangular sponges and give each child one to take home. "Perhaps you can use this sponge to help wash your family's dishes this week."

45

Happy New Year!

You will need:

- three or four obviously new items (It would be helpful if price tags were still attached to one or two of the items.)
- one obviously old item (perhaps an old pair of tennis shoes)

Scripture: (2 Corinthians 5:17) *If anyone belongs to Christ, then he is made new. The old things have gone; everything is made new!*

[Lay out the items you have brought so that the children may readily see them.]

We are going to play a game this morning. I brought several items with me. One of these items is not like the rest. Can you guess which item does not belong here? *[With a small group, give each child a chance to guess and tell why the item he or she picked does not belong. With a larger group, let three or four children guess.]*

If you picked this old pair of shoes, you are right. It doesn't belong with the rest of the objects that are lying here because it is old and everything else is brand new.

I'm sure we all got some new things for Christmas. Don't we get a good feeling when we own something brand new? There's just something satisfying about looking down at our feet wearing a brand new pair of sneakers or riding a shiny new bike that doesn't have a scratch. We've just celebrated the coming of a brand new year. The old year is gone and a whole new year is ahead of us.

In 2 Corinthians, Paul talks about something new. *[Read scripture.]* If we give our life to Christ, Christ will make us a new person. The Bible says the old things go and everything is made new. We can put all our mistakes in the past and start out with a clean slate. As new people in Christ, we want to have fellowship with God; we want to live a life that is pleasing to God. And that is cause for celebration! So let's celebrate!

To take home: Give each child a party popper that reveals a surprise when the lid is removed or a string is pulled. These can be purchased at a party store or through a party/carnival supply catalog. "Before we open the lids, let's say, 'Christ makes everything new. Hallelujah!'"

From Caterpillar to Butterfly

You will need:

- a caterpillar/butterfly "transforming" book (see directions in the "To Take Home" section)

Scripture: (Matthew 17:1-9) [The scripture is told in story form.]

[Show the children the picture of the caterpillar that you have drawn on the "transforming" book.] Who can tell me what this is? That's right. It's a caterpillar. What happens to a caterpillar after a period of time? Yes, it turns into a butterfly. *[Pull the "tabs" so that the transforming book opens to reveal the butterfly.]* The Bible tells about a time when Jesus' body changed the way it looked. Jesus took Peter, James, and John up on a high mountain. While they were there, Jesus changed before their very eyes. His face began to shine like the sun and his clothes became as white as the light. Two other people, Moses and Elijah, who had lived before Jesus, also appeared before the disciples and talked with Jesus. Suddenly, a bright cloud came around all of them, and a voice from the cloud said, "This is my son. I love him and I am pleased with him. Obey him!"

What would you do if you were one of the disciples? Would you be afraid? Well, the disciples became

so afraid that they fell forward on the ground. But Jesus told them to get up and not to be afraid. And when they did, they saw no one except Jesus—the Jesus they were used to. That was a pretty awesome experience, wasn't it? What do you think it showed the disciples? For one thing, it showed them that Jesus really was God's son. It also showed them that when Jesus was with them they had nothing to fear. And these are two important things for us to know, too.

To take home: If you have a small group, you might make a "transforming" book for each child. As an alternative, you could distribute simple butterfly drawings that the children may color and decorate at home. Any small trinket decorated with butterflies (a popular motif) would make a good reminder of the lesson.

How to make "transformer" book:

1) *Fold a piece of typing paper in half, horizontally, and in half again to form a "booklet" that is approximately 8 ½ inch by 2 ¾ inch.*

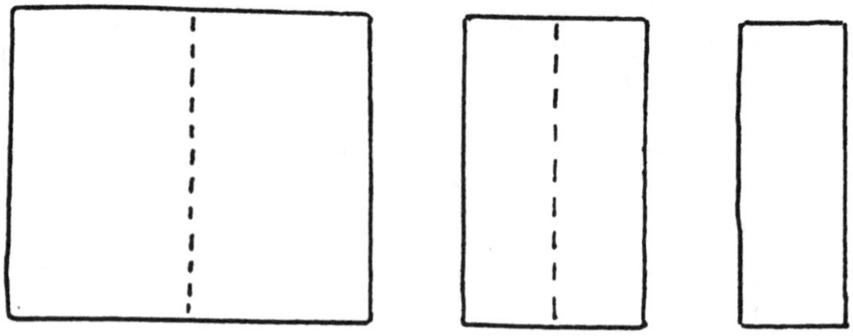

2) *Unfold once and cut three horizontal slits about two inches apart in the middle two sections of the paper.*

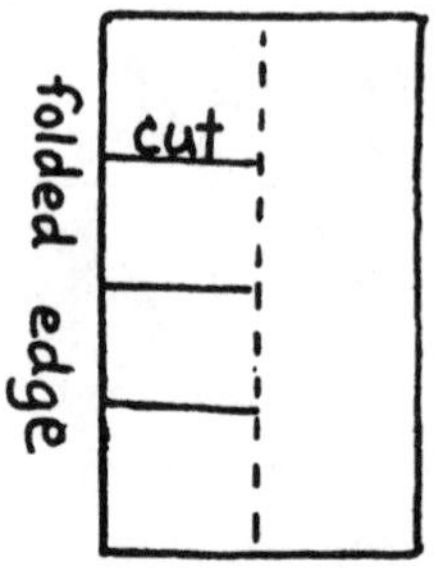

3) *Unfold the paper fully.*

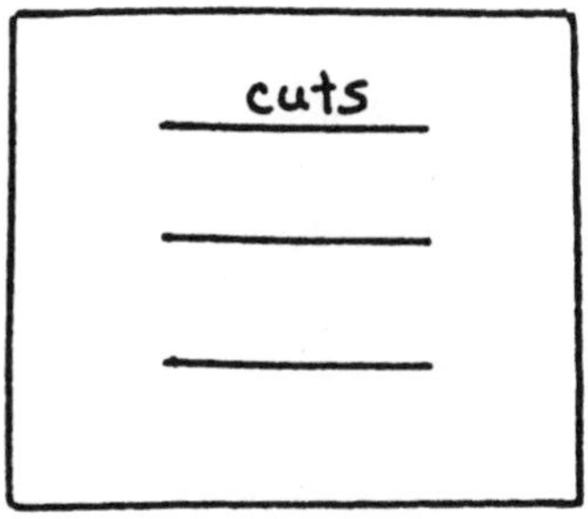

4) *From another piece of typing paper cut two 8½-by-2¾-inch strips and weave the strips through the slits in the first piece of paper.*

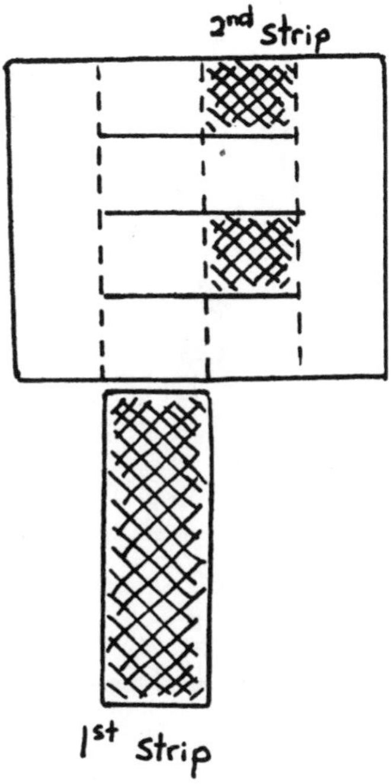

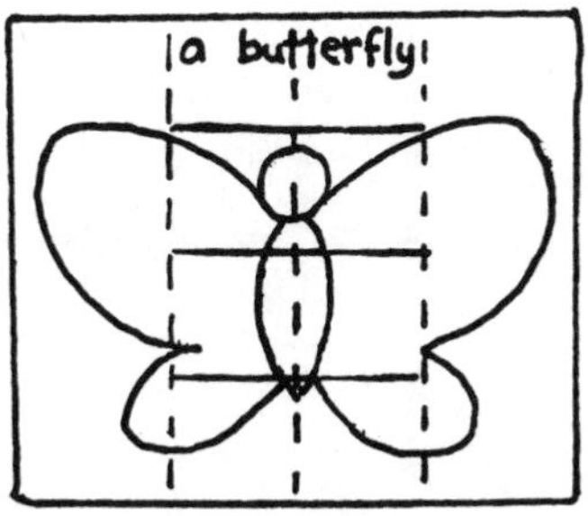

5) *With the woven page lying flat and horizontal, draw a butterfly shape that fills the 8½-by-11-inch space.*

6) *Fold the paper back up on the same fold lines, but this time accordion-style. Then, holding the paper so that the woven section stands upright in the middle and forms a "tent," separate the top of the "tent" (as though it were two "stuck" pages of a book).*

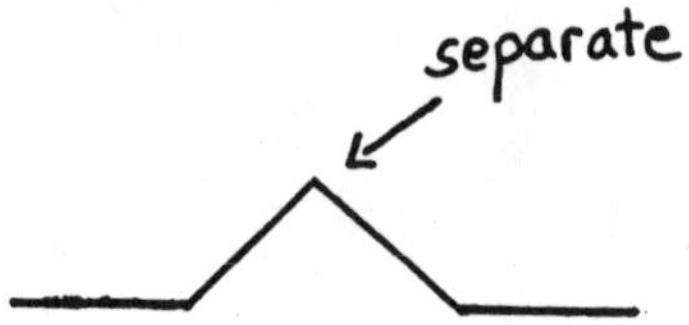

7) *Flatten these pages open so that only the two middle woven sections show. Draw a large caterpillar on this section.*

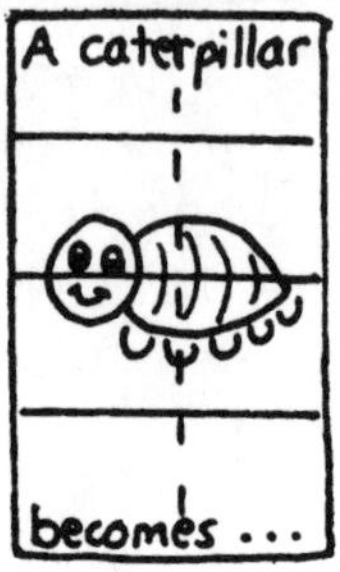

8) *The unwoven edges underneath will become "tabs" that you pull to reveal the butterfly drawing. (For a large group, you might want to make a larger version of the "transforming" book.)*

Note: This sermon is appropriate for anytime, but especially for Transfiguration Sunday.

Scrub-a-Dub

You will need:
- cleaning supplies (rags, window cleaner, feather duster, and so on)

Scripture: (Psalm 51:7) *Take away my sin, and I will be clean. Wash me, and I will be whiter than snow.*

[Display cleaning supplies.] Have you ever heard the term "spring-cleaning"? Maybe your mothers and fathers, or grandmothers and grandfathers get out supplies like these each spring to do a little better job of cleaning the house than they normally do. They might wash windows and blinds or pull out the stove and refrigerator to clean behind them. Maybe they'll clean out the garage or attic.

Christians are now in the season called Lent. Have any of you ever heard that term? Lent begins forty days before Easter and is a time for spiritual housecleaning. It's a time to look inside ourselves to see what kind of dirt and grime has collected—things like bad attitudes, unkind words, and selfish ways. It's a time to say, "God, I'm sorry I've acted the way I have. Please forgive me." It's a time to say, "God, I'm ready to act differently—to act the way you want

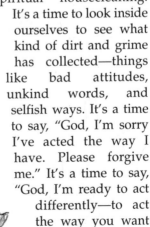

me to act, to think good thoughts, to be kind to others, and to do good and not be selfish."

A long time ago, God's people, the Jews, used ashes as an outward sign of repentance to show that they were sorry for the wrong things they did. Some churches have a special service called the Ash Wednesday service. The worshipers might even have ashes put on their foreheads in the form of a cross as a sign that they want to turn away from sin and act the way God wants them to act.

From now until Easter, during this Lenten season, let's ask God to do some spring-cleaning in our lives.

To take home: Give each child a small bar of soap (you may purchase small guest soaps or travel-sized bars). "When you use this soap, I hope it will remind you of the things we've talked about today. We all can do some spring-cleaning in our hearts."

Note: This sermon is for use during the Lenten season.

48

Even the Stones

You will need:

- a small stone for each child

Scripture: (Luke 19:35-40) *So they brought it [the colt] to Jesus. They threw their coats on the colt's back and put Jesus on it. As Jesus rode toward Jerusalem, the followers spread their coats on the road before him. Jesus was coming close to Jerusalem. He was already near the bottom of the Mount of Olives. The whole crowd of followers was very happy. They began shouting praise to God for all the powerful works they had seen. They said, "God bless the king who comes in the name of the Lord! There is peace in heaven and glory to God!" Some of the Pharisees said to Jesus, "Teacher, tell your followers not to say these things!" But Jesus answered, "I tell you, if my followers don't say these things, then the stones will cry out."*

[Read scripture.] I think what Jesus was saying was that God is so great that it would be impossible to keep all the wonderful things that God has done a secret! If people didn't tell how wonderful God is, then the things God created would do the job.

Sometimes it seems as if the world tries to hide the real meaning of Easter. Sometimes when Easter comes, instead of hearing the story of Jesus, we hear about the Easter bunny or Easter egg hunts or Easter candy. But even if no one in the world remembered the real meaning of Easter—Jesus dying for us and rising again—in a way, the things that God created would "shout" the wonderful news of Easter.

Have you noticed the grass beginning to turn green? Have you seen daffodils or tulips blooming? Have you seen that all the trees are sprouting new buds and new leaves? Easter is about new life—the new life we have because Jesus died on the cross for us and rose again.

To take home: Give each child a small, smooth stone. "I brought a stone for each one of you to take home and to remind you of this story of Palm Sunday. When you look at this rock, maybe it will help you remember the wonderful things Jesus has done and the way all of God's creation shows us the new life that Jesus wants you to have."

Note: This sermon is for use on Palm Sunday.

The Greatest Story Ever Told

You will need:

- a story cube for each child* (gift wrap each cube or put them all in a festive basket)

Scripture: (Romans 6:10, 11) *Yes, when Christ died, he died to defeat the power of sin one time—enough for all time. He now has a new life, and his new life is with God. In the same way, you should see yourselves as being dead to the power of sin and alive with God through Christ Jesus.*

The church has a special Easter gift for each of you today. When I give yours to you, hold it until everyone has one. Then we will all open them together. *[Let them open the gift.]*

This story cube tells the story of Easter. You will see some white arrows on each picture that show which way to open the cube. I would like those of you who can read to read along with me. If you can't read yet, just look at the pictures and listen to the story as we read it. Ready? *[Go through the picture cube, following the arrows.]*

What does this story mean for you and me? If we accept, by faith, what Jesus Christ has done for us:

1. Our sins will be taken away, and we won't have to live a sinful life.
2. We will have life with Jesus while we are on this earth and after we die.

Listen to the wonderful news that Paul gives in Romans 6. *[Read scripture.]*

Let's bow our heads and close our eyes and pray together, thanking God for our wonderful gift. "Thank you, dear God, for what you have done for us through your son, Jesus Christ. Help us live our lives in a way that shows our gratefulness for the gift of eternal life."

To take home: Each child may take home his or her Easter cube.

**Story cubes may be ordered by writing: Good News Gifts, Inc., 1215 W. Baltimore Pike, Suite 5, Media, PA 19063, or by calling: 1-800-300-9831.*

Mother Knows Best

You will need:

- a small gift for each mother in the church (flower, candle, or decorative notepad)

Scripture: (Proverbs 29:15) *Punishment and correction make a child wise. If he is left to do as he pleases, he will disgrace his mother.*

What special day is today? That's right, it's Mother's Day. Mothers are very special people, aren't they? And they are just so smart! Every day, great words of wisdom come from your mothers' mouths. So in honor of Mother's Day, I'm going to read some famous sayings of mothers. As I read these, I want you to raise your hand if you've ever heard them at your house. Ready?

How many times have I told you not to leave your dirty dishes in here?
Get in here and pick up your toys.
What do you think I am, your maid?
Don't talk with your mouth full.
Just taste it.
Eat two more bites of vegetables, then you can have dessert.

You've had enough.
Of course you can't!
Have you brushed your teeth?
Did you go potty?
What are you doing out of bed?
You just had a drink. You can't be thirsty again.
Hurry up!
We're leaving in two minutes, with or without you.
Buckle up.
Quit fighting back there.
Put that down! You could kill someone with that!
Keep your hands to yourself.
Don't make me stop this car.
You did a great job. I'm proud of you.
Turn off the television. You've watched enough today.
You've been on that computer all day.
Go outside and get some fresh air.
Leave your sister alone.
Quit picking on your brother.
Don't make me come in there.
You wouldn't dare.
Stop that! Stop that! I SAID, STOP THAT!
I need a hug.
If I've told you once, I've told you a hundred times . . .
Clean your room; it looks like a pigsty.
Wash your hands.
Pick that up.
That's filthy. Don't touch it.
Don't do that.
One more time and . . .
I've had about enough.
Be nice.
We'll see.
Probably not.
Go ask your dad.

I love you.
What do you mean, you're bored?
Is your homework done?
Are you telling the truth?
I need you to set the table.
Don't argue with me.
Because I said so!
Because I'm the mom!

I know it often seems as if mothers nag a lot. But it's their job to help you grow up to be nice, well-behaved people. Much of the time they're trying to protect you from actions that would hurt you or make you a not-so-nice person. Believe it or not, they say these things because they love you and care about what happens to you. The Bible tells us that punishment and correction by our parents makes us wise. And it goes on to say that if we are left to do as we please, we will disgrace or embarrass our mothers. We should be thankful that God gave us mothers who teach us to do what is right.

Will you pray this Mother's Day prayer with me? "Dear God, help all mothers be the kind of mother you want them to be. And help all children love and respect their mothers because we know this is pleasing to you. In Jesus' name, Amen."

To take home: Let each child take a small gift to his or her mother and then help to distribute gifts to the remaining mothers in the congregation.

51

Fair Fathers, Cooperative Children

You will need:

- a small gift for each father in the church (key chains, nail clippers, packages of nuts, gum, or mints)

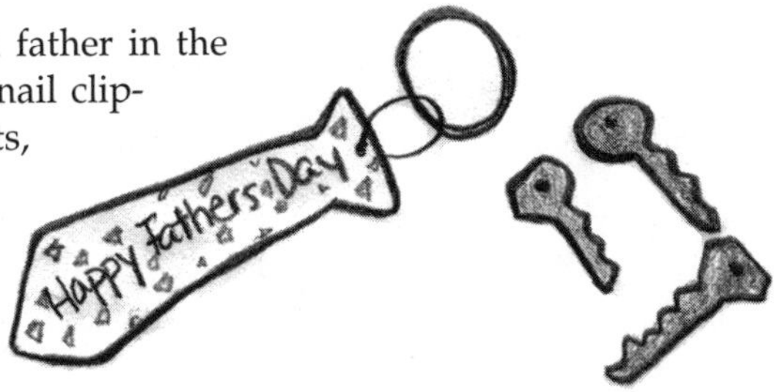

Scripture: (Colossians 3:20, 21) *Children, obey your parents in all things. This pleases the Lord. Fathers, do not nag your children. If you are too hard to please, they may want to stop trying.*

[*Read Colossians 3:20.*] How many of you have heard this Bible verse? When I was a child, it was probably one of the first verses I learned in Sunday school. Have you ever heard your fathers or mothers say that verse? If so, it was probably when you *weren't* obeying them, right? Since this is Father's Day, I want to talk about a couple of verses that apply to fathers and children. Now, listen to this verse: *[Read verse 21.]* Did you know that verse was in the Bible? We don't hear that verse as much, do we? Yet it follows the verse I read first. But as you heard, the Bible has instructions for both children and fathers. You could say that God wants fathers to be fair and children to be cooperative and obey. If fathers and children try to be what God wants them to be, then there will be happiness and peace in the home. When fathers or children go against God's plan, there can be trouble and unhappiness, can't there?

A godly father can help his children understand the love of our heavenly Father. And a godly child brings much joy to his father in heaven *and* his father on earth.

To take home: Let each child take a small gift to his or her father and then help distribute gifts to the remaining fathers in the congregation.

52

God's Gift of Love

You will need:

- a "Birth of Jesus" story cube*

Scripture: (John 3:16) *"For God loved the world so much that he gave his only Son. God gave his Son so that whoever believes in him may not be lost, but have eternal life."*

I have a Christmas gift for each of you from the church. It's a story cube about the birth of Jesus. Please wait until everyone gets one before opening yours. The white arrows show which way to unfold the cube. Let's read it together. If you can't read yet, look at the pictures and listen to the story as we read it. *[Read through the picture cube.]*

What a wonderful gift we have received—God's only son! We receive this gift because God loves us so much and wants us to live in heaven forever. Maybe you can share this story cube with someone who doesn't know the real meaning of Christmas.

To take home: Each child may take home his or her Christmas cube.

**Story cubes may be ordered by writing: Good News Gifts, Inc., 1215 W. Baltimore Pike, Suite 5, Media, PA 19063, or by calling: 1-800-300-9831.*

Index of Scriptures

Topical Index